Praise for

The Pursuit of Grace

It was as if Kristen ran beside me to gently plead for a change of course. I saw myself running for self-fulfillment, chasing after lies, seeking false identities, hiding my trauma, and trying to be everything but His. Kristen reminded me what the race is truly about and Who is actually running to me!

—Logan Cates
Minister at Durant Church of Christ, Durant, Oklahoma

I found myself completely drawn into Kristen's story, letting the truths she discovered sink in deep. In her book, *The Pursuit of Grace*, she invites us into the freedom that is found when trauma, shame, and brokenness no longer define us. These pages hold a message of hope, helping readers find their way to the source of true identity, self-worth, and lasting freedom.

—Christi Slaton
Senior Creative Director of Product Development, DaySpring

The Pursuit of Grace is a must read for anyone crumbling under the pressure of perfectionism. We live in a world where words like vulnerability and authenticity are great catch phrases, however, the majority of the population is terrified by the reality of it. Anxiety and depression are fueled by comparison to others and the desire to measure up, or even worse, our own self-loathing and judgment. *The Pursuit of Grace* not only gives us connection to others through their stories of vulnerability but also gives us useful strategies in embracing our own brokenness and living vulnerably and authentically in the light of God's grace. I highly recommend this book for anyone struggling

with rejection, shame and fear of being truly seen by the God who loves them.
—**Ashleigh Rakestraw** Master of Science in Social Work (MSSW), Licensed Clinical Social Worker (LCSW)

I wasted years of my life pursuing this illusion of perfection and secretly holding a world of pain inside of me. I was too afraid to fully come before the Lord or anyone else with the deepest places of hurt, or fear, or failure, or trauma, or imperfections living inside of me. This book hit deep places in my soul. It gave me permission and encouragement to uncover hidden hurtful places and helped me allow myself to continue to surrender to the heart of the Trinity. As I read *The Pursuit of Grace,* it helped me grasp the grace of our good Lord and Savior. Receiving and standing under His grace is one of the best things we can spend our life pursuing. Don't spend another second void of His grace. Read this book and fully allow yourself to work through your hurt, pain, burdens, trauma, fear, failure, and brokenness alongside the loving God who made you and knows you deeply. This book will be a catalyst for your healing, transformation, and growth. This book aids in binding you even more so to the heart of the Lord.
—**Ny McNeely**
Former Minister and Author of *The Word Living and Active: A Guided Journey Through Scripture*

There is healing and grace for all who have been broken and held hostage by their fear of vulnerability and the surrender of control. There is a place of grace created by Christ where we are invited to stand and from which we are allowed to live. *The Pursuit of Grace* encourages us to enter into this grace God has so richly provided and to be transformed by it. Through her own vulnerability, stories of grace, and insight into the Scriptures, Kristen humbly invites us to join her on the journey that leads to a grace-filled life.
—**Sam H. Pace**
Minister, Mission Point Church of Christ, Westminster, Colorado

THE PURSUIT OF

~~PERFECTION~~
Grace

KRISTEN LUNCEFORD

Published by KHARIS PUBLISHING, an imprint of
KHARIS MEDIA LLC.

Copyright © 2023 Kristen Lunceford

ISBN-13: 978-1-63746-210-2

ISBN-10: 1-63746-210-7

Library of Congress Control Number: 2023933489

All KHARIS PUBLISHING products are available at special quantity discounts for bulk purchase for sales promotions, premiums, fund-raising, and educational needs. For details, contact:

Kharis Media LLC
Tel: 1-479-599-8657
support@kharispublishing.com
www.kharispublishing.com.

Table of Contents

Acknowledgments

First and foremost, I would like to praise the Lord for His never-ending pursuit of me. I would not be the person I am, nor have the relationship with Him that I have, without His loving patience and extended arms ready to catch me when I fell. I am forever grateful.

Next, I would like to thank my husband, Adam. It is not easy to appear in a book that highlights your mistakes, but his desire to give hope to the world superseded his shame. He is a true minister of hope, not only to his family, but to everyone around him. I thank him for the strength he provided me to write this book, and the encouragement to stay strong. Thank you, Adam, for staying up late with me while I read you each chapter. Your heart is selfless and kind. I love you, always.

I would also like to thank my parents for continually being a source of strength for me. They have devoted their lives to their children and have forever impacted us because of it. I am thankful for their godly examples in faith, love, and grace. Thank you for reading my book with me and helping me stay on track!

Last, I would like to thank all those who shared their stories with me and had the strength and trust to let me write them down. Again, it is not easy to display your hurts, trauma, and sin to the public but, my dear friends, you were willing to do just that in order to give hope to a hurting world. Thank all of you who contributed to this book and encouraged my soul.

Introduction

Grace. I'm not very good at it. Receiving it, giving it, understanding it; it is a difficult concept for me. Growing up, I had always heard the word *grace*. I had heard the standard definition of "unmerited favor," but my understanding of it stopped there and it was hard for me to internalize. Even in writing this book, I've had to look at the meaning several times. Grace: The free favor of God and bestowal of blessings.

It's the free part that gets me, probably because you and I know that nothing in life is ever free. There's usually a call for sacrifice, dedication, or hard work. "Free" goes against our natures.

As a perfectionist, I like the idea of knowing that if I work hard for something, I can achieve it, I can obtain it. I like having control. I like being able to make my life be a certain way, look a certain way, and function in certain ways. None of that comes free, but rather from my perseverance and determination. With those character traits, I can succeed.

I deserve what I work for. Perhaps that is why I never understood grace, because I was always seeing it as something I had to work for, something I could earn by my merit. My definition looked more like: *Grace: the favor of God and bestowal of blessings based on my accomplishments.* I didn't understand how to live in something that came freely; I equated grace with perfect living. If I *appeared* to live perfectly, succeed perfectly, and raise a family perfectly, then I was worthy of the *free* gift. That was an illusion. There was no perfection behind any of it, only an attempt to portray it to the world. Grace was such a foreign concept and, therefore, not a huge part of my faith system at all. In my life there was no room for mistakes, no room for disorder, no room for chaos, and subsequently, no room for grace in its true form, as God intended.

The day finally came when I was ripped from the comfort of my supposed perfection. Everything was falling apart. I felt like I was trying to put shattered pieces of glass back together and I had no idea where to start. Suddenly, I was faced with chaos, disorder, and brokenness, and it was difficult to cope. I was faced with imperfection when all I had ever pursued was perfection. *How do I even live in such a world?*

The answer I came up with? *Fake it. Pretend like I have it all together, like I have everything under control, and then perhaps I will.* The answer came unintentionally; I didn't know that was my answer until I took a step outside and peeked in. I had been living my life in constant pursuit of perfection so long that when my life was less than perfect, I felt the need to keep up the image of it. I could not accept myself as broken, and even if I was, no one needed to know.

If you are anything like me, you like your life like I like my car. With four kids always on the go, I have to admit, we eat in the car quite a bit. However, being a perfectionist, I am also somewhat of a neat freak. Okay, more than somewhat. I like us to eat in my car without anyone knowing we eat in the car, so I constantly vacuum it, wash it (I'm the weirdo with the monthly car wash subscription), and always have the kids pick up anything they brought with them into the car. I do not like clutter. I do not like messes. I make sure my car has the constant scent of country apple, cherry pie, or something delicious and apparently edible, to mask the haunting scent of fast food and stinky soccer socks.

Now, if you are thinking I sound crazy, I get it, but the truth is, this is exactly how we like to live our lives. While there are messes throughout our existence, we don't want people to know it. We will work tirelessly to vacuum up any trace evidence of a mess to appear as if there never was one! We like to be in control: in control of our successes, our failures, our marriages, our children and, therefore, our value. When things are out of our control, it can be humiliating, humbling, and easy to lose our sense of worth. When our value is tied to our perfection, but failures come, it is easier to vacuum the crumbs and act as if they were never there.

The problem with this mentality is that it begins to be a prison. If we live pursuing this life of perfection, we will always be a slave to it. When things seem perfect, we feel great, when things are not perfect, we feel useless, but we must pretend like we feel great. So, we become silent sufferers hiding behind a wall of smiles. It is in those moments that depression sets in for so many, and it did for me as well. I felt the need to keep up, but I couldn't, so I faked it, slowly dying inside.

I didn't think anyone could relate or understand, and I believed no one would show mercy. I couldn't experience the healing of grace because it was always associated with my perfection. I had never realized that grace was *in* the imperfections, that the imperfections were *necessary* in order for me to understand the Lord's pursuit of me. In fact, it has taken thirty-eight years for me to realize that He has been running after me since the day I was born. The Lord knew that pursuing perfection was in my nature, so He pursued me with His nature—grace—knowing the whole time that I would become desperate for it. It was because of His undeserved love, even in my brokenness, that grace came running after me.

It is in the soul-crushing moments that we all have a choice to make. We can choose to pursue the image of perfection, display it to the world, and let it imprison us, or we can surrender our broken pieces, live in authenticity and choose to be defined by the healing grace of God, His undeserved love and blessings. I can say this for sure—one is more freeing than the other.

This is my story of learning to live a life defined by grace, coming to terms with all of my hurts, trauma, and sin, and surrendering it all to the Lord. It has been a difficult journey. It has been a journey that has changed my life.

I pray with all my heart that you will join me on this journey. Let us throw off the temptation of being defined by our successes, people, our circumstances, or sin, and learn to be defined by the undeserved love of God. The journey may not be pretty, it may be chaotic, but in the end, the pursuit of grace will change us all.

Chapter One

A New Reality

I sat on the edge of the bed in the guest room of my house, where I had slept the night before. I'd had my suspicions for over a year but could never convince myself of the certainty of it all. I didn't want it to be true, so I ignored the obvious signs until I could ignore them no more.

All the time I had spent alone during that past year, all the indifference towards me, and even more, all the annoyance in response to my very presence at times, was starting to point to the truth. This truth I had tried so hard to overlook was being laid out right in front of me by my dad, who had more courage to face reality than I did.

He was looking at me, tears in his eyes, and quietly spoke the words, "Your husband has something to tell you." He didn't have to. I knew. These were the words I was dreading to hear, the words I knew in my heart to be true but wished with all my soul that they weren't. You know that feeling when your world seems to stop spinning, yet everyone else's continues? The feeling that everyone else is moving forward with their picture-perfect lives and you are left behind, picking up the shattered pieces of yours? This was the day my world stopped spinning.

My heart sank to my stomach; my whole body seemed to ache as I listened to my husband's confession of an affair. I heard his words but was overwhelmed by the pain. My worst fear was emerging as fact. I'd played this out in my head, Hollywood style, multiple times. I knew exactly what I was supposed to do in this moment: After his confession I was supposed to deliver some clever line as I walked out the door, immediately causing him regret that he had ever let me go. My real reaction was quite different: There was no clever line. I had no desire to walk out the door. I loved him, and all I wanted in that moment was for him to love me back.

His gaze was fixed on his feet; our eyes didn't meet. No matter how hard I tried to look for any sign of connection, it never came. Everything seemed distant and taciturn. I had never felt more alone than I did in that moment. All I could hear, all I could internalize, was that he had chosen someone else. I had been rejected and exchanged. I wasn't enough. I suddenly felt small, pathetic, and disposable. My confidence had been ripped out from under me. The lump in my throat barely allowed me to swallow, let alone speak.

I had overwhelming feelings of betrayal and anger; even more, I felt a contradictory desire to run into my husband's arms and seek refuge, but I couldn't. *How could he protect me from heartache when he is the one who caused it?* A thousand questions rang in my head, causing complete insecurity, isolation, and a sense that the life I knew was over. The only words I could manage were directed to my father, "What about my babies?"

I was four months pregnant with twins, planning to be a stay-at-home mom, and was now at a complete loss. *Where could I go from here? I had been replaced, discarded, and abandoned.* The dreams I had as a young wife and mother were shattered.

We all set out with dreams when we are young, dreams of endless possibilities, exciting adventures, and perhaps even romance. We tend to find our identities in those dreams and endeavors. Some aspire to be doctors, some teachers, while others may be lawyers, social workers, or go into the military to serve their country. What we become, becomes our identity; what we are successful at gives us value. If we are doing great at our jobs, we have value; if our kids are successful individuals, we have value; if our marriages are picture-perfect, we have value, and if we fit in socially, we have value.

If this is true, however, then we believe the converse must be true. If we are not good at our jobs, we lose value. If our kids are not successful, if our marriages aren't perfect, if we don't fit in our environment, if our picture-perfect lives come crashing down, we must not have any value. This is exactly how I had lived my life to that point.

❧❧❧❧❧

Growing up, I had a wonderful family: two loving parents, three brothers, and two sisters. My parents were devoted to their faith and made sure that we attended worship three times a week, rarely missing a service. My family was involved in ministry, church activities, and leadership.

We didn't just claim a faith, we lived it. I'll be honest and say that I think that contributed to my struggle with perfectionism. My parents worked so hard to become the reputable family we were, and I began to see their success as a way of gaining admiration. I witnessed the way people respected my family and I wanted that. I wanted to do good, be good, and be admired for it. Of course my intentions were innocent; I was not aware of my desire. I believed in being good and doing good, but I was now equating it with my performance. I believe that tainted the way I grew up thinking about God.

As I grew in my faith, I saw my works and my achievements as something that would win peoples,' therefore, the Lord's affection and admiration. He must be proud of me because I go to church three times a week, I'm kind to people, I don't see bad movies, and I don't use bad language. As I got more involved in teaching Bible classes, starting Bible studies, and volunteering, I saw myself as even more worthy in God's eyes. I was worthy of God's love. The more I did, the more I was loved, and the better I felt.

It is interesting to me to see how much that way of thinking affected my faith because my faith was built on the idea that I could earn God's favor. I could earn His love and grace, so I worked tirelessly to do all the right things, but for all the wrong motives. Hints of self-righteousness began creeping in. I was becoming proud of myself. Honestly, I was not all that different from a Pharisee. My words and my actions all pointed to God, but my heart did not. I was doing the very thing Jesus cautioned against in Matthew 6:5, "And when you pray, do not be like the hypocrites, for they love to pray standing in the synagogues and on the street corners to be seen by men." I was saying prayers for all to hear with hands held high for all to see.

In my mind, all the "good" I was doing became deserving of grace, love and admiration, not just from the Lord, but from everyone. This mentality began to affect the way I saw myself, the way I saw people, the way I saw the church, and the way I saw the Lord. What I worked for became what I deserved and what defined me. If I worked hard at school, I would get good grades and be considered a good student (unfortunately that was not what I worked hard at, and it showed). If I worked hard at relationships, then I would have them and be loved. As long as I was doing the things that were respectable, I would be respected.

Eventually that train of thought carried through to my marriage and parenting. If I was wise in choosing the right person and worked hard at my marriage, then it would be successful, I would be a good wife, and I would earn the respect of others and of the Lord. If I worked hard at raising smart, independent, and successful children, then I would be a good mom and I would have value. Beginning in my childhood and growing-up years, I had believed that if I was doing well in life, I was worthy of love—love from people and love from God, and I carried that with me until the moment I could no longer carry it.

Here I was, sitting before my husband and the Lord, with nothing but imperfection. I had nothing worthy to offer anymore. Throughout my life I had never accounted for failure, mine or others'. I never accounted for mistakes, for broken people, or for sin, which begged the questions, *Who am I if things are not perfect? Who am I if I fail at school, if my relationships fail, or now even my own marriage? Even more so, how could God still love me even when I was falling apart?* I was not performing as I believed I should, so where was the respect and admiration now? Because I was living in the pursuit of perfection, I had let it define me and give me my worth. But now? I had just lost it all.

In such dark moments, we often struggle to come to terms with our identities when the only identity we've known has been stripped away. We realize we are not everything we thought we were. When we live our lives in this pursuit of perfection, we don't know how to cope with failing. Oftentimes, we try to cover up the imperfections and keep on going; we display our best selves to the world because we crave that acceptance and admiration too much.

When imperfections are revealed, we are scared to display them to the world; it is too easy for others to judge, too easy to misunderstand, too easy to condemn. We place the burden of performing on ourselves and we crumble under the pressure of trying to keep up. We believe the lie that there is no value in the wounded and scarred. As for me, I couldn't even come to the Lord with my imperfections; I was too ashamed that I had them at all. I had worked so hard to get it all right, but I failed. I thought surely the Lord must be as disappointed with me as I was with myself, probably more.

I believe that most, if not all, of us experience this type of awakening in one form or another. I will never forget having a conversation with a woman I had just met at an event a few years after my own heartache. Her eyes were puffy, her hair unkempt, and her soul destroyed. She was in her late fifties, her children were grown and gone, and her husband had recently decided to leave her for someone younger. She was devastated. In tears, she asked, "If I am not a wife, and I'm not a mom anymore, then who am I? I have no role, no identity."

She spoke the words that terrify many who fear ever relating to them. All of us long to fit somewhere, to be needed, to have a purpose and a source of value. The thought of losing our place in this world is enough to send many into the deep throes of depression and suicidal thoughts.

It can be terrifying, exhausting, and tempting to resist, but it is in those moments that we have a choice: to let our imperfections define us and so constantly live in the pursuit of perfection, or to surrender our broken pieces and be defined by the healing grace of God. There comes a time when everyone must face the broken pieces of their souls and redefine their source of value.

A few years ago, my son, who was about seven years old at the time, was swimming in our backyard with some family friends. Later that day, I realized I had not seen my son in a while, but I figured he was so busy playing that I must have just kept missing him. When I finally caught sight of my sweet boy in the kitchen, I went to give him a hug and tell him I loved him, but as I approached him, I saw a look of fear in his eyes, and I couldn't understand why. He reluctantly gave me a hug and tried to hurry away. That was it.

I knew something was wrong with my usually loving and cuddly son. He was absolutely avoiding me. I asked him if he was okay and he replied with a quiet and reserved, "Yup." It was obvious he wasn't okay. Upon further investigation, and finding dried clumps of blood in his hair, I discovered that he had hit his head in the swimming pool and split it open. He had gone in the bathroom to clean up the blood, and then hid behind a wall for over an hour to conceal the wound. He had split his head down to his skull, desperately needed stitches, but didn't want anyone to know about his wound. When I asked him why he had not come to me, he responded, "I knew I had hurt myself badly and I didn't want to go to the hospital. I thought they might give me a shot."

That night I could not sleep because I kept thinking about how my son did not want to come to me in his pain. He chose to portray happiness when he was wounded and bleeding. I wanted so badly to be his place of refuge. I wanted to be his source of healing and comfort, but he was too scared to reveal to his own mom that he even had a wound.

As I lay there in bed, I realized that this is exactly how the Lord must feel when we do not come to Him in our brokenness, when we choose to be defined by our wounds, yet hide behind a mask. Instead of being defined by our healing, we are defined by our broken pieces. We try to silently, clean up our blood, and conceal the wound, when we're really making it worse. Isn't this the same battle that Adam and Eve had after they were exposed? Instead of running to God in their moments of weakness, they scrounged up the only thing they could find to cover themselves: fig leaves. They were so ashamed of having a weakness that they couldn't even come to the Lord for healing. They sought out their own remedy, completely bypassing the One who could truly provide.

If only there was a way to surrender our imperfections and seek our definition from the One who can heal all wounds. We need a Master Healer and, oh, how He longs to heal us, but that means we must be willing to be vulnerable. Our desire for healing must surpass the shame we feel for needing to be healed. We cannot hide our wounds; we must let Him see them. When we do, there may be pain in fixing them, but it will be the most perfect healing.

It is a tragedy to me that there are not more stories of perseverance, repentance, and redemption. Instead of posting our successes and our accolades, we could be digging deep into the lives of real people and witnessing the true healing power of God. Why aren't we listening to the people who have been knocked off their feet and learned how to recover? People in the church are being tested and tried and are overcoming through the power of God, but they may be so afraid to reveal their battles, retreating in shame that they even had a battle to begin with.

I have done this very thing. I get it. Judgment from others can be cruel and is enough to cause you to want to live in a cave the rest of your life. When you already feel pain, why open yourself up to more? It's easier to smile and just pretend there was never a battle in the first place. We choose even the perception of perfection over the healing grace of God.

It is with this mindset that we stifle the story of redemption to the world. In fact, this suffocates the very breath that gives life. What does it tell the Lord when we deny our brokenness? As I think about the many people Jesus healed: the paralytics, the demon-possessed, the blind, and so forth, how ridiculous would it have been for them to tell Jesus, "I do not need to be healed, because I am not broken."

What if they were so ashamed of even needing to be healed that they claimed they weren't in need of it at all? Jesus came to seek and save the lost, the sick, and the broken, but we are preaching that our salvation and identity come from our pursuit of perfection. When that is our message to the world, we proclaim that there is no room for deficiency. There is no power working in weakness. There is no healing. It is best to just pretend to be strong.

Paul, however, had a different point of view in 2 Corinthians 12:9b-10. He said, "Therefore I will boast all the more gladly about my weaknesses, so that Christ's power may rest on me. That is why for Christ's sake, I delight in weaknesses, in insults, in hardships, in persecutions, in difficulties. For when I am weak, then I am strong."

For Paul, his hardships were a necessary part of his ministry: to testify how God works in a broken world and how God heals people. Brene Brown once said, "Grace means that all of your mistakes now serve a purpose instead of shame," (Liles, 2002). That was exactly what Paul was testifying to. People need to know that living in the grace of God means embracing your imperfections and the power of God that they can display. Your life is messy, but it doesn't define you. You are loved unconditionally, and there is healing in that. God can work His best in our weakness. If we are so ashamed of our bruises and scars that we cover them up, we are covering up the very grace of God working in them.

The Lord tells Paul in 2 Corinthians 12:9, "'My grace is sufficient for you, for my power is made perfect in weakness.'" That statement begs the question, if I am *not* weak, is His grace sufficient or am I? If I am not weak, is His power being made perfect? If I am *not* weak, and Christ is *not* strong, then there is no hope for anyone out there who is hurting and feeling weak. There is no remedy for our struggles.

However, if I *am* weak, and Christ *is* strong, then anyone out there who is struggling has hope, and it is in the very name of Jesus. It is in the moments of life that knock us down, when we feel abandoned, useless, and hopeless, that we testify the loudest to who God is and what he can do. Whether we hide our wounds or reveal them, we testify something about God. Either he is a rescuer and healer, or he is not. The broken pieces of our lives do not need to be hidden, but revealed, so that the true, grace-giving nature of God can be seen. That truth is essential for the rest of the world to know. When we choose to live in grace, we choose to let the power of Christ be seen.

It is through the grace of God that I can say my husband and I are still married and have been for sixteen years. Both of us made the difficult decision to redefine our source of value. We chose to dig deep into the Word so that we might see ourselves the way the Lord sees us. It took years of counseling, years of stripping away our old ways of thinking, and a lot of self-reflection and dedication to living out the love and forgiveness of the Lord. It has taken a lot of patience and a lot of practice to develop a love founded on the grace of Christ. We realize we are broken together and we stand on level ground at the foot of the Cross. We have four beautiful children, and we are forever grateful for the life in which the Lord leads us. We wouldn't have it any other way.

It is the power of God that saved our marriage, and we are so thankful for His dedication to us. For years we allowed ourselves to be defined by our story, so we hid it, but now we are choosing to be defined by our healing and we pray that in revealing it, you find hope that you also can find your value in His grace, His undeserved love. We do not want anyone to feel like they don't have a place, or that their story is something to be ashamed of. We want everyone to know that God can bring beauty from ashes, and that the world *needs* to see that lived out.

Throughout this book I have followed not only my story, but the stories of others whose realities and self-perceptions flipped, crashed, disintegrated, or otherwise changed. I have changed most of the names to protect those involved. I am so thankful for their willing hearts to reveal hope to the world. Every one of us has had difficulty accepting the dark, twisted paths our lives have taken due to shame or fear of rejection, but chose instead to live in the pursuit of perfection to those around us, believing we could keep up the act.

It wasn't until we all reached a breaking point, where we could no longer live in the lonely and chaotic lies that we sold, that we comprehended our need for rescuing. The charade was over. We were all called to a life of surrender to the One who could provide ultimate healing in our imperfections. We no longer chose shame in our weaknesses, but rather glory; glory to the One who creates beauty from ashes.

We chose to live in a life with no shame, but rather pride that the grace of God extends to our very selves so that we might help others realize the grace extended to them. If God can work in me and the others in this story, then He can certainly work in you. We are not alone. We can surrender together and be freed from our shame of brokenness.

Chapter Two

Prepare To Be Broken

Growing up, I was a dreamer. I was the girl in the corner of the classroom with the dazed look on her face, fantasizing about my future instead of focusing on the math problem. Who needs math when you have dreams, right? If you can dream it, you can achieve it! While I never felt the need to listen to my teachers, the desire to become one was in my blood. It is what I always wanted to be. Since my kindergarten years, I knew I wanted to mold and shape the lives of the future generations. Nobody would be dazed in my classroom; it would be the ultimate learning experience.

After returning home from a long hard day at school, I would force my brothers and sisters to complete the "fun" math pages I had created and make them sit in my homemade schoolroom that was our dingy basement, while I taught some well-thought-out lesson on life. They wouldn't admit it, but they had a great time.

As I got older, my dreams unfolded. I knew that after teaching a few years I wanted to be married, have several kids, and eventually be a stay-at-home mom. I looked forward to the days of cleaning my own home (there's that weird side to me again), making my kids' lunches, making meals for my husband, and reveling in my role as the perfect wife and mother. As a young woman, it was fun to dream. It seemed that anything was possible and exciting to think about, however, in all my days of dreaming, it never occurred to me that my dreams could not happen, that maybe I wouldn't become a teacher, find a spouse, or be able to have children. I had no backup plan; I didn't even think I would need one. Perfection came from performance, and I could perform. I would perform.

I mentioned in the Introduction that I am a perfectionist. I like things to function in certain ways and be organized in certain ways. Being a perfectionist, I am also a planner. I like things to be focused, purposeful, and timely (I know I must sound like a blast to be around). Plans equal safety. Plans equal stability and calm. Without a plan, there is nothing but chaos.

Have you ever tried to plan a vacation with people who are not planners? They like to just get there and wing it, no reservations, no schedule, no plan; they thrive on the anxiety-producing thrills that come when they don't know what's next. Me? That's enough to ruin a vacation. Who wants to escape the craziness of life just to live in the anxiety of vacation chaos? Nope, I like to know exactly what I'm doing, how to get there, and where we're staying. The most exciting unknown venture is where we will be eating dinner.

Luckily, I married a man who is the same way, so when planning vacations or any outing we both search for the most structured way to go about it. We know how we will get there, what we will do, the cost, the time it will take, and when to get back and how. This is how I live my life: according to the plan. It should come as no surprise that it is really what my dreams morphed into: a plan. It was my mission. My only mission. In time, I graduated college, got married, started my teaching career, and was on my way to motherhood. I was living life according to the plan.

I don't think I am alone in getting swept up into dreams or plans. I think we all do. We dream up the perfect job, the perfect spouse, the perfect place to live, the perfect amount of income, and anything else that could give us hope and a future. It's not a bad thing.; I think it is what keeps us going, but problems begin to arise when the plans get derailed if we dream it and do not achieve it. We never plan for that. We can probably all think of a time in our lives when we made plans and nothing went as planned. Weddings became a disaster, birth plans were foiled, jobs moved us to different states, and relationships failed. These stories make for excellent table conversations but experiencing them is a whole different event.

I remember a time in my childhood when my parents had planned a weeklong vacation for all eight of us to Six Flags® in Texas. We were all so excited and could hardly wait to get there. My parents had the whole thing planned: our flight, our car, our hotel, our itinerary, and our Six Flags® tickets, but when we arrived at the park, the parking lot was completely empty. That's never a good sign at an amusement park. It was closed for the week. Apparently, they had been doing renovations.

My parents hadn't even thought about the fact that it might be closed. Who would? In all their hard work of planning, they didn't plan for the one thing that foiled it all. That's life. Sometimes, no matter how well we plan, it just doesn't come together, and it's when our plans fail that we have the most difficult time recovering.

This was certainly the case for me. Looking back on all of my dreams and plans growing up, I realize that perfection was my mission. I never intended it to be, but it became that way because all of my dreams became my expectations, my purpose for living. Everything I did was centered around accomplishing my mission. I believed if I worked hard enough, everything I planned and dreamed would happen.

The problem is that life simply does not care about the plans we make or the dreams we have. It does not take into account our hard work to accomplish what was needed. Life just happens and as perfectionists, this can be a hard pill to swallow. We like control; we like a say over how our lives should turn out. When we are in control, our lives are all about us: our dreams, our plans, and our wants, which slowly morph into our demands. Those become what we believe we deserve. We demand the life we have worked so hard to accomplish, and when it doesn't happen, we don't know how to thrive outside of that. When we are not in control, our dreams, our plans, and our wants mean nothing. We can make no demands, and we don't like that. To us, that seems the recipe for an unsatisfying life.

As I began to write this chapter, I kept thinking of my Aunt Marcia. I wish I could introduce you to her; there's just no justice in words. She is a woman I have always admired because of her quiet strength. She is a precious soul and one of those people who make you feel seen and heard in any conversation. Her wisdom exudes out of her and draws you in. She's the kind of person you could just sit and listen to all day, the person whose testimony changes you. For me, she has been the living example of being thrown by the instability of life.

Marcia married Dave in her early twenties and had two sons, Dustin and Caleb, followed later by their sister, Carrie. They bought their first home in Palm Desert, California, were active in their church, and always had people over for fellowship. They loved camping, serving in the congregation, and going to 7-11™ on Friday nights to let the kids pick out three sweets for the evening movie or game night. Marcia and Dave dreamt of the lives their children would live as they grew. They dreamt of having grandchildren and growing old together.

A month shy of turning thirty-two, Marcia faced unspeakable tragedy. The boys, who were seven and nine, along with their dad Dave, were packing up for a fishing trip to Yellowstone National Park. Excited and armed with their new knives and fishing poles, they hopped into the car without any kisses and hugs for their momma. Little did she know that would be her last memory of them.

As they approached the end of their fishing excursion for the day, a terrible storm came, the boat capsized and threw everyone into the water. Tragically, her husband, Dave, and their two sons died that day. They were a month and a half short of their thirteenth wedding anniversary. One day she was sending her boys on a father-son adventure, full of excitement, and just a few days later they were all dead.

After receiving the horrifying news, Marcia remembered the last words Dave spoke to her, "I love you and everything's going to be all right, Momma." But it wasn't. In one night, she became a widow, lost her two sons, and was forced to find a way to make it on her own, supporting her only surviving child. Her table of five had suddenly become a table of two. The once noisy home filled with running and laughter, was now quiet and nearly empty. There would be no more anniversaries, no more date nights, and no growing old together. The dreams of their future were gone.

As if that wasn't tragic enough, not able to make enough money, she was forced to give up her house and her car, filing for bankruptcy shortly after. This was never part of the dream. She was forced from the dream life into a nightmare. How could there ever be a plan for something like this?

While most of us would be completely derailed by a situation like this, my aunt had a different reaction. Oh, she was distraught and heartbroken, to say the least, but she was able to embrace her loss of control and use it for something far greater.

In a conversation we had recently, she said, "I've had many people over the years ask why God would let that tragedy happen to me, and my answer is always, 'Why not me?'" In a time when most people would be overcome by the thoughts of, *why me,* her response was completely the opposite.

I'm going to let that sink in for a moment.

After losing her husband, her sons, her house, money, and safety, her response was, "Why not me?" Most of us spend our lives trying to hold on to whatever piece of control we can grasp, trying everything we can to avoid pain. We become angry when we are forced to experience it, but here she was, embracing her trauma. She was devastated yet dedicated to living the life God called her to. She was not seeking control, she was giving it up. She was the complete opposite of me.

In listening to my aunt's testimony, I began to understand that in all my planning I had made my quest for perfection my mission. It was what I was living for. I was expecting the best because I was doing my best. My life had always been about me. Aunt Marcia, on the other hand, was living for a different mission. She was not living for the glory of herself; she was not demanding the life she believed she deserved. Her mission was rooted in something much deeper. Her identity and value did not come from the dreams she was fulfilling, but rather from the life she was using to give testimony. Christ was her mission, and the tragic pieces of her story were a vital way to point others to Him.

At a conference where Marcia once spoke, she encouraged young girls to dream. They should dream about their futures and hope for sweet things to come, but in all of that, she implored them to make *Christ* their mission, not to make their dreams the mission. When our dreams and our plans are our mission, we become incensed at anything that might derail that, and we spend the rest of our lives in pursuit of making it right. That's what I did. When Christ is our mission, the storms don't derail us, but rather we use them to testify to the Lord's deliverance.

Oh, those storms can be painful. It will be heartbreaking and wearisome, but we embrace the opportunity to testify to the power of God working in it. James 1:2-4 says, "Consider it pure joy, my brothers, whenever you face trials of many kinds, because you know that the testing of your faith develops perseverance. Perseverance must finish its work so that you may be mature and complete, not lacking anything." If our mission is to preach Christ, then our perseverance through storms is what will preach the loudest. The storms become *essential* to the mission. Yet when perfection is our mission, we can only view storms as inconvenient and disruptive to a life well lived.

I would say most of us start our lives expecting the Lord to live for our mission instead of our living for His. It's all about us. All of our planning, efforts, and dedication are focused on how to make our personal lives better and more convenient. We expect God to comply. It's no wonder we get disappointed, frustrated, and depressed when our plans don't work out. We believe we deserve more and are owed more, even without realizing it. We were never promised a heaven here on earth, but many of us come to expect it. With this mindset, storms become deluges that send us off into delusion that causes us to question whether or not God is even with us.

We see in Job 29:4-5 that as Job began to suffer his own loss of family, health, and wealth, he seemed to fall into the same delusion. He cried out, "Oh for the days when I was in my prime, when God's intimate friendship blessed my house, when the Almighty was still with me and my children were around me. . . ." Job assumed that because he was experiencing a storm, God was not with him; that the intimacy between them was gone. Job equated peaceful living as intimacy with God, when really it was the opposite. The Lord was at work in the storm! Job was so focused on pursuing his own justice and restoration, that he failed to see the necessity of the storm. He missed the opportunity to testify to the power of God working in it all. When perfection is our pursuit, we will miss the experience of God working in the storms. We will fall into the delusion that God is not with us, when really, we are not with him.

Perhaps we need to refocus our dreams and plans. If we started out in our early years learning to seek the mission of Christ, instead of our ideas of perfection, we could begin to prepare for the ministry. Like my Aunt Marcia, we could learn to embrace the storms as a way to testify to the One who can deliver us from them. We would no longer see our suffering as an inconvenience and a disservice, but as a part of our mission.

One of my favorite stories in Acts is when the apostles began testifying to the mission of Christ, they were arrested and brought before the Sanhedrin. Because of their testimony, they were flogged and ordered to no longer speak. Acts 5:41 says, "The apostles left the Sanhedrin, rejoicing because they had been counted worthy of suffering disgrace for the Name." They were not horrified or repulsed at their call to suffering, but rather rejoiced in it. How could they rejoice in being flogged and persecuted?

I believe it is because they were living for something outside of themselves. Their mission, their dream if you will, had changed. They no longer lived to fulfill themselves, but lived to glorify Christ, no matter how difficult it became.

Kristen Lunceford

Every one of us is going to face a challenge of some sort, or we already have. We cannot escape it. We must be prepared. I wish I could say I had prepared for this mission to glorify Christ my whole life, but I hadn't. I was living for a different mission, which is why, when my life fell apart, my pursuit of perfection only worsened. I was trying to remedy something that could not be remedied. I was not Christ-centered. I thought I was trying to root myself in the Lord, but because I was so focused on myself, I didn't root myself very deeply. I thought I was living the life the Lord called me to, but I was only living the life I called myself to. I was not Christ-missioned; I did not see my trial as a testimony to be used for Him, but as punishment for something I didn't get right.

I was like Job's friends who thought disaster came upon him for something he had done wrong. They kept telling him to repent of whatever sin he had committed so he could get back into the good graces of God. Without realizing it, that became my own conviction. I believed that trials or trauma happened because people were not quite where they needed to be spiritually. My mission was always myself and my performance, so it's no wonder I wasn't prepared for the storm.

In the most recent discussion I had with my Aunt Marcia, she offered some words of wisdom that she speaks to anyone who will listen: "To prepare for the storms, we must be anchored in the Word." It is only through the Word that we will have the strength to live the life God is calling us to. It may not be an easy life, but it will be a life with a purpose, a purpose outside of ourselves.

Since we are called to live a life of testimony, we must be anchored in something strong enough to withstand the suffering that comes with it, and our striving for our own perfection isn't it. Only through the pursuit of the Lord will we be able to withstand anything that comes our way. Our ways become His ways. Our thoughts become His thoughts. Our strength becomes His strength. It is critical to fill our souls with the words of the Lord if we are to accomplish any mission.

My dad and I were recently talking about this very thing, and he began to make a beautiful comparison to a ship setting out to make a voyage. As you push off the dock, it is a beautiful calm blue sea. You can smell the salty ocean air and feel the sun hitting your cheeks. As you get further out, a small dark cloud begins to appear, seemingly no threat at all. It is in this moment that you have a choice: you could batten down the hatches, tie down the cargo, and bring in the sails before a storm hits, or you could wait to see if a storm actually comes and then prepare.

Unfortunately, that is often what we do. We live out our day-to-day lives pursuing our own missions when a storm seems to hit out of nowhere. Unprepared, we enter the storm unsecured. How much better would it be if we prepared for the storm *before* it happened? Instead of quickly opening to Job and Psalms to weather the storm that's already occurring, what if we were anchoring ourselves *ahead* of time to the very strength of God? I bet the storm would be a very different experience.

The second piece of advice Aunt Marcia gave was to get rooted in the church. It was the church that had stepped up to provide for her and her daughter, Carrie, living out the instruction given in Romans 12:13, "Share with the Lord's people who are in need. Practice hospitality." They provided meals, financial help, and emotional help. They were her source of comfort and healing.

We were never meant to carry our burdens alone, but so many of us in the crisis of a storm retreat instead of engaging and lightening our burdens. As the early church developed, we see in Acts 2:44-47 that the believers "were together and had everything in common. Selling their possessions and goods, they gave to anyone as he has need. Every day they continued to meet together in the temple courts. They broke bread in their homes and ate together with glad and sincere hearts, praising God and enjoying the favor of all the people." The church — the first members of the body of Christ— were reliant on one another. They were serving Christ in action, edifying and lifting each other up. Why? Because life gets hard. Life gets lonely. The Lord in all His goodness knew this and prepared for it by creating the church. The church was His heart being extended to those He loved who were being called to a difficult life. It was all a part of God's plan.

Rooting ourselves in the Word and in the church are God's foolproof plan to help us prepare for the storms that a life lived for Christ will certainly endure. With the Word, we have the power of God working in our hearts; with the church, we have the power of God working through others. We are not setting sail alone. With the anchor of the Word and the crew of the church, our mission is in focus and we can be prepared for the coming cloud in the distance, but if we have neither of these we are sailing into the storm, unsecured and alone.

In Philippians 4:11-13 Paul says, "For I have learned to be content whatever the circumstances. I know what it is to be in need, and I know what it is to have plenty. I have learned the secret of being content in any and every situation, whether well-fed or hungry, whether living in plenty or in want. I can do everything through him who gives me strength."

Because Paul was living for the mission of Christ, he was willing to endure whatever came his way because it was testifying to the power of God working in people, and he was able to endure it because of the strength the Lord gave him. Anchored in the Word, we gain the strength to complete our mission. If our mission is to teach, we will do so in the strength of the Lord, and if it is not to teach, we will do so in the strength of the Lord. If our mission is to marry and have children, we will do so in the strength of the Lord. If our mission calls us to lose our spouse or children, we will do it in the strength of the Lord. Being anchored in who God is and what He can do will give us the strength we need to endure whatever mission He calls us to.

Heeding my Aunt Marcia's advice, it is time to start preparing for storms. If you are in a storm, get anchored. If you are not in one, get anchored. And after you are anchored, become a crew member on someone else's ship to ensure their survival as well. Our mission is simple: Christ and Him crucified. Secure the ship, batten down the hatches, tie down the cargo, and bring in the sails. There is a cloud in the distance, and if we aren't anchored in Someone stronger, the storm will surely overcome us.

Chapter Three

Running to Escape

I was twenty-five years old when the affair was revealed to me. When it all came crashing down, I believed I was in the prime of my life, living a dream. Shortly after that terrible day, I was sitting with my parents in church, dreading the announcement that was coming. I could not focus during the service, which seemed to drag on for hours, slowly torturing my mind with anticipation. I wanted all of it to be over, not just the announcement, but all of it. In fact, I wanted it to have never occurred in the first place.

Because of our involvement in the church, the nature of the affair, and to suppress the rumors, we decided to reveal the truth of my husband's affair to the congregation.

Rumors can be even more cruel than reality. I was terrified, humiliated, and heartbroken. I knew full well the hurtful comments that could emerge in situations like this. I was dreading the "well-intentioned" advice, opinions, and judgments of others.

Before leaving for worship that morning, my dad gave me five smooth stones to hold; he had once held them during a difficult time in his own life. The stones were a reminder to let God fight the battle. I rubbed the stones together during the service and thought of David, who wholeheartedly believed in the saving nature of God, and how he ran at Goliath full force, without hesitation, sling in hand, ready to conquer with his stones.

I was not ready to conquer. How could I run at this full force, with full faith, when I didn't want to admit there was a battle? I wanted to be out in the fields, peacefully shepherding sheep, not facing the greatest enemy. I didn't want to fight—I wanted to run.

I think that most, if not all, of us have a little bit of the runner in us, not for a lack of faith, nor a waning love of God, but rather when we reach a point in our lives when breathing is the only next step we can take to stay afloat. We become desperate for respite and it becomes vital to look for an escape route that will provide some type of relief. It's understandable. We often take on our battles alone, so they are heavy burdens that may eventually become unbearable.

When we reach those moments, it becomes necessary to find relief, to escape, but if there is no solution in sight, we run. Sometimes, we run to unhealthy relationships, alcohol, money, or addiction; sometimes we run by isolating ourselves from those around us. We run to or from something, but either way, we are running.

After our reconciliation, my husband Adam and I quickly moved our new family of four to Arizona. We did not know a soul; no one knew what we had just experienced, and that was how I wanted it. I was living life at surface level, nothing beyond, nothing deep, nothing painful, nothing real. Every Sunday we showed up to church, dressed in our Sunday best, smiles on, children neat and tidy, sitting perfectly in a row. We got involved in worship, Bible studies, book clubs, and even made our house available for use. From the outside, we looked like an ideal family. On the inside, I knew the truth. I knew I was a runner. I was a broken person in need of healing, but instead of turning to the Lord in my time of brokenness, I fled.

Because I was not ready for a storm, I was not ready to testify through it. I was ashamed of it. I wanted no one to know that ugly part of my past. It was embarrassing, shameful, and easy to judge. I craved the admiration; I craved the idealistic lifestyle; I craved "perfection." It was how I had always defined myself, so without it, I had nothing.

For eleven years, I kept my past a secret, believing that if anyone knew, they would be ashamed as well. You, dear reader, might be able to relate to that. I bet that most of us hide our messy secrets. Why? Because it's hard to be genuine. I think it is part of our nature to always put our best foot forward, believing that showing any signs of weakness is actually weakness itself, and believing weakness is something to be ashamed of.

It takes intentionality to be genuine; it does not come naturally to most. I think we all can relate to walking in the church doors, asking the typical questions, "How are you? Did you have a good week?" and expecting, sometimes hoping, that the response will be a simple, typical response. We don't want to dig deep, we just want to extend courtesy. Anything beyond that sends us out of our comfort zone. We like to ask clean and simple questions and receive clean and simple responses.

We get uncomfortable when others seek to share genuine confession, and we certainly wouldn't share our own, but we portray to others that everything is under control. There is no room for people whose lives are not in control, and if there is no room for people with broken lives, where do they fit in the church? The truth is, they don't. It's too messy, it's too difficult, it's too much drama. Well-intentioned or not, when we all pretend that we have it all together, we kick out the ones who don't. There will never be room for the broken as long as we keep our messes hidden.

In 2021, an art piece called *Can't Help Myself* went viral. It was designed by Sun Yuan and Peng Yu and consisted of a constantly moving robotic arm, gently scooping hydraulic fluid that was spilling out from itself all over the floor. In the beginning, it was easy to scoop it all up, so when it did, the robot would celebrate with a dance. As time progressed, the robot had to work harder to clean up the mess that was rapidly spreading. Eventually, there was no time left for the robot to dance—it was enslaved to the life of cleaning up the mess it had created. Red fluid had splattered on the windows and walls, and the floor had been stained. It was not a beautiful creation anymore; it was messy, run-down, and falling apart.

In time, the robot could no longer keep up. It had worked so hard trying to keep it all neat and tidy that it could no longer function at all.

The robot stopped. The tragedy is that the robot did not even need the hydraulic fluid. It was electric, so it spent its life cleaning up something it couldn't use and didn't need. The robot already had its power source but lacked detection for it. When I watched this video, I found myself tearful. Sounds a little hokey, but it is true. The robot got me; I could relate to it. Perhaps you can, too.

The truth is, no matter how hard we try to clean up our messes, the stains will remain. There will still be splatter we can't reach on the windows and the walls. We will never do enough or be enough to fix the damage, but we were never intended to. The pressure we feel to do that has come from ourselves. We are constantly looking to the right and to the left, comparing ourselves to the "perfection" we see all around us, and we always fall short. We are disappointed in ourselves for not being enough or doing enough, so we live in a constant cycle of trying to fill the gaps. We exhaust ourselves to death pursuing something we were never meant to pursue, something that will never provide life. The robot did not need hydraulic fluid. We do not need to portray perfection. When we live our lives in pursuit of "being enough," we are denying our very source of life. Being enough is not attainable and therefore does not produce life. The cross does.

A few years ago, when my husband and I were headed to a date night, we received a phone call just as we pulled up to one of our favorite restaurants. When my husband picked up the phone and put it on speaker, it was Nick, someone we had known for years, someone who had chosen the more difficult paths on his journey. There was desperation in his voice; words were coming out so fast it was hard to internalize what was really going on.

We knew he was driving, we knew he had a gun, and we knew he wanted to end it all right there. Sitting in our car, we felt completely helpless as we were states away, but we blurted out any words that might convince him to hold on a little longer. As his story began to unfold, we realized he was in trouble. The decisions he had been making finally caught up to him, and there was no escape. He did the only thing that felt familiar to him; he ran.

Nick grew up an energetic young boy. His family nicknamed him, "the Tasmanian Devil" because he was always busy and always on the move. When he wasn't roaring like a dinosaur, he was running like a lion. In fact, it was his rambunctious personality that eventually caused him to feel different from his mild-mannered siblings and peers. While all his siblings seemed to be the pictures of perfection as obedient children, Nick struggled to fit the mold. Rules were made to be broken; silence was made to be interrupted, and calm was torture to his soul.

His siblings began to resent Nick's personality. From the time he was young, he was always the boy on the outside looking in. His brothers and sisters would laugh, tell secrets, and play games, but rarely extended an invitation to Nick., He was too much to handle, too much to take in, and just too much in general. Nick believed the only solution to his problem was to conform, but it seemed that no matter how hard he tried, he just couldn't do it.

After years of pursuing this perfectionistic "normality," Nick became exhausted. Holding conversations was difficult, reading the room was difficult, and trying to fit in was impossible. He was tired of trying to talk less, mess up less, and just be less. It was easier to become the rebel he was seen as and to thrive in it.

At fourteen he ran away, and he would spend the next twenty years constantly on the run, trying to find acceptance. There were marriages, there was drinking, and there was addiction. For two decades, Nick was in pursuit of whatever could numb the pain of rejection, but he never could. He spent so much time pouring himself into people and things that would never pour back into him. The pain was getting worse, the decisions were getting more desperate, and the consequences were sprinting after him. It was in these moments that he found himself driving up a mountain, gun in hand, ready to end the misery.

We don't have to look very far to see the phrase, "You are enough," posted on coffee mugs, T-shirts, and backpacks. While I completely understand and respect the sentiment, I think it causes a false sense of reality. Society constantly tells us we are not enough: we are not rich enough, pretty enough, skinny enough, accepted enough, and after all that, life tends to provide sufficient evidence to prove we are not enough.

So why do we spend our lives trying to be just that—enough? What if there could be joy in not being enough? What if we could find peace, satisfaction, and value in accepting the difficult parts of our lives, instead of running from them? What if God's grace truly was sufficient and not just a verse we posted? If we could learn to accept the twists and turns in life, and let God's undeserved love of us be what defines us, not society or life, perhaps it would bring the freedom we all crave.

We cannot keep everything together all the time, but just like the robot, we do not need to. We do not need to waste our lives chasing something that provides us no life to begin with, but only imprisons us. The reality is that we often do just that. We tend to run from trauma, chase the dream life, post that to the world, and imprison ourselves within it. The truth is that ultimate healing will not come until we embrace the life we have, damages and all, and begin using it for the glory of God. When we deny that any good can come from the stains and brokenness, we deny the power of God, who works in all of it. We proclaim to the world that God cannot work in imperfection, and that His grace is not sufficient for us or anyone else.

As our conversation with Nick progressed that night, we were finally able to talk him down the mountain to face the demons he believed were coming for him. The consequences would not be easy, and would involve jail, halfway houses, and loss of home and freedom. Once again, he was going to feel the pain of being an outcast, but this time, he was being called to face it. Through intense therapy and recovery, Nick was able to step outside of himself and take a look inward. After several tests, it was confirmed that Nick suffered from bipolar disorder—primarily manic; obsessive-compulsive disorder (OCD); attention deficit-hyperactivity disorder (ADHD); post-traumatic stress disorder (PTSD), and traumatic brain injuries (TBI). There were finally causes for what he (and others) believed was "wrong" with him. There were reasons he was different.

The difficult part is that he had to learn to accept those mood, anxiety, and neurological disorders within himself. He had to come to terms with his differences and the ways he put people off. Somehow, he had to learn to be okay with who he was, even if others weren't. Over time, he slowly began to address his pain of rejection as a child, to verbalize his need for affection, love, and acceptance, and to give himself grace to see his own actions as an attempt to make himself whole. It was a painful journey, but he was learning to let go of the opinions of others and define himself in a significant new way.

It was in this time of life that someone asked Nick to join him in Bible study. Nick had grown up in the church; he knew all about God, but it was obvious that he didn't really *know* God. There's a big difference between the two. Many of us can go through our lives going to church and learning *about* God, but it is a different story to *know* God intimately, to know His character, His heart, and His desires.

Through this Bible study, Nick was called to see the Lord in a different light; not as a far-off God who expects obedience or else, but rather, as a pursuer. He was called to see himself as one pursued by a God who was chasing after him, longing to fill every hole and broken place he'd ever had. He encountered the Bible as an incredible love story, a story of a God who longs to dwell with His people, and even in their constant rejection of Him, pursues them with His grace.

Through Bible reading and study Nick began to see his worth to God. He began to see how the Lord had pursued him throughout his life, all while he was running to be filled by something else, somewhere else.

It was the story of Hagar that captured his heart. Remember Hagar? It's okay if you don't, because we often tend to overlook her story, but I'm sure she was used to being overlooked. She was the servant of Sarah and Abraham. Abraham and Sarah were promised a child, but it took a long time for the promise to come true, so Sarah, in her desire for a child, decided to give her servant Hagar to Abraham. (Perhaps Sarah, too, struggled with pursuing fulfillment in her own way). Instead of accepting the position to which God had called her, she chose to take control but her pursuit outside of God led to problems between her and Hagar.

Genesis 16:6 says that Sarah mistreated Hagar, who ran away into the desert, a place where there is no hope. In her jealousy of Hagar, Sarah rejected her and Hagar ran from her rejection. Sarah needed perfection, and expected perfection, but Hagar wasn't cutting it. The beauty of it all is that God's grace found Hagar anyway. Verse 7 says, "…the angel of the Lord *found* Hagar" (emphasis added). He was intentionally looking for her. He didn't stumble upon her; he didn't just happen to see her wandering around in the desert. He found her.

In the midst of Hagar's hopelessness, the grace of God was looking for her. The Lord met her where she was, in her broken state, and made a promise to fulfill her. At the end of their encounter, verse 13 says, "She gave this name to the Lord who spoke to her: 'You are the God who sees me,' for she said, 'I have now seen the One who sees me.'" Hagar named God El-Roi, the "God who sees." I love that. The God who sees me. She was broken, rejected, and ran to escape, yet out there in the desert, in her darkest moment of despair, she was seen by the God who sees.

This is what Nick desperately needed: for God to see him, not through the lens of perfection, but seen just as he was, broken. Dwight L. Moody said, "Grace is undeserved kindness. It is the gift of God to man the moment he sees he is unworthy of God's favor," (Rodin, nd). It is in the very moment we recognize our brokenness that grace comes running, chasing after us to give us the hope of everlasting worth. For the first time, Nick began to see a glimmer of hope, hope of living life as himself, with the pursuing love of God to define him. While he thought he had to pursue perfection, and when that didn't work, he pursued the pain, but he got it wrong the whole time. God's grace was pursuing him! In his imperfections, in his sin, and in his pain, grace was looking for him. After experiencing a life of rejection, the thought of God pursuing him was life changing.

What is interesting about Hagar's story is that in Genesis 16:9, after her encounter with the Lord, God called her to go back to Sarah. Hagar was being asked to go back to the source of her rejection, so that God could fulfill His promise. I'm sure she questioned how going back to such a painful place would have any role in God's fulfillment of her, but the Lord knew she needed to be redefined. She needed to face her source of rejection with the newfound knowledge of being seen by the One who sees. He wasn't asking her to be whole, He accepted her broken pieces and promised that He would make her whole. In recognizing God's pursuit of her, she was called to see her situation differently. That was what Nick needed, to go back to the source of his rejection, but this time, instead of letting it define him, he turned around and into the loving arms of grace embracing him. After all this time, Nick could stop running; grace was in pursuit.

In his book, *Knowing God*, J. I. Packer says, "I am graven on the palms of his hands. I am never out of his mind. All my knowledge depends on his sustained initiative in knowing me. I know him because he first knew me and continues to know me. He knows me as a friend, one who loves me; and there is no moment when his eye is off me, or his attention distracted from me, and no moment, therefore, when his care falters," (Taylor, 2016). The Lord has always been in pursuit. We are always in His heart and on His mind. When we are out wandering in the desert, we can be sure God is out there searching for us. It is because He first knew us and began His pursuit long before we ever knew of our need of Him, that we have an identity. We need to let ourselves be redefined.

In Genesis 21, we come to the end of Hagar's story. Unfortunately, it gets worse before it gets better. Sarah was still not living out the grace of God and kicked Hagar and her now young son out into the desert again. Another rejection. As she and the boy reached the end of their food and water, hopelessness reared its ugly head. They cried out and in verses 17-19, "God heard the boy crying and the angel of God called to Hagar from heaven and said to her, 'What is the matter Hagar? Do not be afraid; God has heard the boy crying as he lies there. Lift the boy up and take him by the hand, for I will make him into a great nation.' Then God opened her eyes and she saw a well of water. So she went and filled the skin with water and gave him a drink." As Hagar was sent out in the desert, once again, the Lord was right there and heard their cries.

The first time in the desert she was seen, the second time she was heard, and what did God do? He showed Hagar that she was never out of His heart, that she was never off His mind; He had provided all along. It says, *God opened her eyes to the well that was there* (v 19). She had been so focused on her desperation that she missed it. We do that. It is too easy in our moments of desperation to run, to let the pain of rejection overwhelm us. We miss the opportunities to witness the provisions of the Lord because we are too busy running.

I still get tearful reading Hagar's story. It is beautiful. It is my story; it is Nick's story, and I'm sure it is the story of some of you. Nick and I had forgotten to come to the Lord in the time of our complete rejection. We tried to fix it and survive on our own when the solution was always there in front of us. We just needed our eyes opened. Without even meaning to, we can easily push out the true Rescuer and pursue deliverance elsewhere, but we will never be delivered.

When we allow our eyes to be opened, we see God for who He really is and can then see ourselves for who we really are. If we serve a God who sees, hears, and delivers, then *we* are seen, heard, and delivered. There is no need for anything else. God's grace is enough.

At this point I just want to encourage you that if you have gone through a time of rejection or trauma, please know there is a God who sees you, hears you, and wants to deliver you. Let Him show you the well of life. He has already provided for you. It's time to stop running.

Chapter Four

The Pursuit of Perfection

103 lbs., was my ideal weight. It might seem like an odd number to get stuck on, but the only explanation I can give is that there is no logic in insanity. Any higher and panic, self-loathing, and depression would kick in. Over the passing months I was becoming more aware of the rejection I had just experienced from the affair, and my self-worth began to decrease.

After having my children, I would see my reflection in the mirror and be flooded with disappointment. I could see why no one would want me. I had fallen far from "perfection." I was not the exciting, adventurous, playful girl I used to be. I was exhausted, untrusting, and introverted. I was overwhelmed by my feelings of unworthiness.

Within a few months of my time in Arizona, a few months into my new, shiny life, a familiar feeling of desperation had come, except this time no one knew about it. I was hiding under smiles, laughter, and a picture-perfect family. I was a slave to the mask I was wearing, all in the name of perfection. I was desperate for relief. I was desperate for escape. I was desperate for self-worth.

When living under the mask of perfection, our feelings of unworthiness spread like a disease. We can only see ourselves the way that we feel, broken. We are not able to keep up with the demands of perfection, so it only intensifies our self-loathing. When we say the wrong things, mess up our dinners, gain a little weight, lose a friendship, or let the house become a disaster, we let it add to our unworthiness and the need to just get things right.

We are choosing not to be defined by the unconditional love of God. We choose to live for conditional love, and we feel the need to perform. That is exactly what I did. I could not accept myself as broken, in need, or inadequate, so instead of turning to unconditional love, a love that chooses me despite the ugly, I turned to conditional. When we choose not to live in grace, we choose not to give grace to ourselves. We will always be trying to make up for our insufficiencies and punishing ourselves as part of making ourselves right.

That is what I had always known. Perhaps if I worked hard enough, I could have that worth and value back. I just needed to perform.

I began exercising to "feel better" (but really to feel better about myself). I had always said that the only reason I would run was if someone was chasing me, and even then, I wasn't sure it would be worth it. But desperate times called for desperate measures. And I was desperate. Running turned into biking, which turned into boot camps, which turned into private classes and private training.

I became obsessed, exercising multiple hours a day, five days a week, sometimes six, and as I saw the numbers on the scale fall, I was hooked. I wanted more. I could finally take control of the life that had spiraled out of control. The thinner I was, the more valuable I became. I made sure to eat no more than the number of calories I burned exercising that day, because in my mind, if I burned more calories than I ate, then it was like I didn't even eat at all, and any extra calories burned throughout the day were gold. My weight was falling rapidly, however, the high from the new numbers on the scale quickly diminished when I walked away feeling the constant pangs of hunger, but it was worth it.

The thinner I became, the better I felt about myself. But not for long. Inside I was miserable. Inside I became angry. I was angry at my husband for eating whatever he wanted, whenever he wanted, and without a care. I was angry that I even felt like I needed to lose weight. I was angry at myself for believing that I could somehow find my worth in my weight, something I *knew* to be wrong, but still found myself drawn to. I hated going to restaurants, movies, coffee shops, and people's homes because it was like a torturous display of everything I could not eat.

I became resentful when I made cookies, pancakes, or anything yummy for my family because I couldn't have any. I wanted so badly to eat, but I wanted 103 lbs even more. When I struggled to find value in my weight, I partook of more options from the conveyor belt of dissatisfaction like shopping, makeup, hairstyles, and anything superficial that I thought could bring me value, but never did.

I am going to pause here for a second. I am choked up and fighting back tears as I type this. I am heartbroken that this was my reality. It is embarrassing, humbling, and tragic to me. This is never the person I wanted to be. I loved the Lord with all of my heart, and I am so sad that I chose to not be defined by His gracious love. It is painful, it is not pretty, but it is the truth. I exchanged the grace of God for a lie, the lie that I was in control of my self-worth.

If only I had accepted the Lord's view of me, through His never-ending, always faithful love, instead of focusing on what I believed I lacked. His definition of me is filled with so much more grace than I was willing to give myself. It is gut-wrenching to think that the Lord was there all along, just waiting for me to give it all up and rest in the presence of His perfection and complete acceptance of who I am. If only I had just surrendered my worth to Him.

When we go through life-changing experiences, it is hard to not let it affect the way we view ourselves and we are drawn to find a way to fix it. We want to be whole and to be seen as whole, and when we experience something that alters that, we are prone to find something that will fill the void.

When I think about the garden of Eden, I can't help but think of the perfection that it must have been, a green oasis in the middle of the desert. I picture lush, green trees dotted with red, orange, blue, and purple from the fruit they bear. I can imagine exciting sounds of the lions roaring, the exotic birds singing, and monkeys howling. There is a morning mist to water the gardens, and a river flowing through the middle, a refreshing spring for man and animal. I can see animals roaming around in the stillness of the day, living in harmony with man. There is no fear, no sadness, no pain, and no death, just perfection, a utopia, if you will. On top of all of that, there is the very presence of God, perfection himself, walking in the garden in the cool of the day. There is absolutely no need for anything else.

Somehow, breaking through the walls of perfection, the voice of a serpent caught the attention of Eve, filling her with doubts that this type of perfection could ever really satisfy.

"Did God really say, 'You must not eat from any tree in the garden?'" The woman said to the serpent, 'We may eat fruit from the trees in the garden, but God did say, "You must not eat from the tree that is in the middle of the garden, and you must not touch it, or you will die."'

'You will not surely die,' the serpent said to the woman. 'For God knows that when you eat of it your eyes will be opened and you will be like God, knowing good and evil.'" Genesis 3:1-5

In the midst of perfection, a voice called out. It is hard to imagine that anything inside this garden could possibly be deceiving, but it was. Satan was there, ready to destroy the innocent ones whom God had created. Filling Eve with doubt, Satan was able to persuade her to pursue completeness outside of the Lord. It wasn't hard; it started with just a lie, a lie that Eve wanted to believe and it's the same lie we all fall prey to: "You can be like God." Perfection. And with one bite, humanity entered into a never-ending spiral of discontentment, chasing a god-like role we were never meant to have.

Now there was absolute fear, absolute sadness, absolute pain, and absolute death. Eve was no longer satisfied with the glory of perfection walking in the garden with them, loving them as they were, but rather chose a life of chasing her own perfection, one that would never come. She wasn't looking to live amid the grace of God; she wanted to *be* God.

Kristen Lunceford

While we often look at Eve as the weak-willed woman who sent humanity to its demise, the truth is, we are all Eve. We all make the same choice she made. At one time or another, we all face doubt and choose to pursue the glory of ourselves rather than the glory of God. It is in our weakest moments that Satan begins to do his work in us. He tells us that we are not complete as we are; we can be more and do more, and then he makes it sound like a great thing. It sounds like a tempting invitation to self-empowerment, something we see preached all around us in society. With a little more money, we can be happy. With a little more success, we can be complete. With more relationships, we can have self-worth. With acceptance, we can finally belong. *We* can create the life we want; *we* can make our life perfect.

But perhaps it's the life we were never intended to live. Perhaps perfection is just dwelling in the midst of grace, knowing that you don't have to keep up, that it pursues you, chooses you, just the way you are. Maybe we need to change the definition of perfection. Perhaps perfection is being defined by the One who doesn't need our own. Maybe perfection is grace.

Tragically, sometimes walking in the garden with the Lord is not enough for us; we want more. However, when we pursue these calls outside of the glory of God, we are only deceiving ourselves. Eve was so blinded by her desire to be like God that she could not see the lie for what it was. It was dressed up as an innocent need: wisdom. The problem is not that she was seeking wisdom; it was that she was seeking wisdom outside of God. By tasting that fruit she thought she could provide her own wisdom and provide her own value. She could provide her perfection. We do that. With the same innocent intentions, we listen to the same lie and pursue value outside of God, whether it be through money, success, relationships, belonging, our spouses, or even our children. The problem is we nor anyone or anything else cannot make ourselves worthy or valuable. It will never be enough. When Eve's eyes were opened, they were opened to her own desperation, to her own lack of godlike abilities.

Eve did become wiser, but it was to the fact that she was broken and in need of rescuing. Instead of turning to the Lord when she took that bite, she quickly remedied the situation by covering herself with leaves, believing that somehow nothing had changed. She took control of the situation instead of giving it up. When we take control, all we do is become more aware of our inability to make ourselves whole. Eve could never be enough, never have enough.

In fact, all of humanity would come to that realization. We will never be enough. It was the Lord, in whose presence she had been living, who had been her source of value the whole time. He saw her as she was and loved her anyway. There was nothing she needed to change about herself; she was his, and that was perfection.

In the same way, it is the Lord who is our source of value. There is nothing that God expects us to "fix" about ourselves. He simply wants us to come, surrender to our need for him, and let his grace change our lives. When we can finally see ourselves the way that the Lord sees us, we can't help but have it change our lives. When we search for value outside of the Lord, it will always fluctuate and will ultimately reveal our lack of worth. We are only chasing an image we perceive as completeness, and we will quickly realize that it is an image we will have to constantly pursue.

This mentality has been around since the beginning. Since Eve, we have always been looking for ways to replace God. Romans 1:21-23 reveals, "For although they knew God, they neither glorified him as God nor gave thanks to him, but their thinking became futile and their foolish hearts were darkened. Although they claimed to be wise, they became fools and *exchanged the glory of the immortal God* for images made to look like mortal man and animals and reptiles" (emphasis added).

In the time of the Israelites, all nations, including, at times, some of God's own, rejected God as their perfect source of life, and pursued their own idea of perfection. They worshiped creation instead of the creator. Whatever they wanted, they pursued, no matter the cost. They, like Eve, rejected perfection, to *become* perfection themselves. However, as Romans 1 states in verse 25, "They exchanged the truth of God for a lie." They could never be the image of perfection. Nothing they desired to have or be would ever satisfy. They, themselves, could never be enough. God knew it all along; he tried to warn them, but they just weren't willing to listen.

As I was reading through my Bible this year, something stood out to me more than it ever had before: the number of times the Lord had been rejected or exchanged for other gods. It was a tragic realization. I often think about the cross as the ultimate example of rejection, so I've glossed over the others, but as I read through this year, it hit me hard the number of times the Lord had been rejected in Scripture.

The Israelites' entire relationship with God had been riddled with the rejection and exchange of Him. If the surrounding nations had kings, the Israelites wanted kings, no matter that God was their King. They would be delivered by the Lord from enemy after enemy and then build golden calves and claim that *they* were the source of deliverance. They would trust in their numbers of horses and chariots instead of trusting in the name of the Lord their God. They did anything they could to replace God with something else. Whenever they were faced with their own perceived imperfection, usually by comparing themselves to other nations, they would immediately remedy the situation with a person, idol, or possession, a replacement for God. When I read about the habits of Israel, I can't help but see myself. I'm inclined to seek refuge in things or people that just cannot give it, and in turn, I'm always in search of something that can.

In Psalm 135 we see an excellent comparison of the replacements we choose versus God. "I know that the Lord is great, that our Lord is greater than all gods."

Why? It goes on to say in verses 6-14 that the Lord makes the clouds rise; he sends the lightning and brings out the wind. He struck down Egypt, performed signs and wonders, vindicated his people, and provided compassion. In other words, *He acts!* He is not a god that sits idly by. He is always on our side, working on our behalf. One of my favorite passages is after the Israelites had just been delivered from their bondage in Egypt.

They have been released, have come upon the Red Sea, and are now being chased by the angry and revengeful Egyptians. In their distress, they cry out to the Lord, and this is His response in Exodus 14:13-14, "Stand firm and you will see the deliverance the Lord will bring you today. The Egyptians you see today will never see you again. The Lord will fight for you; you need only to be still." God is always working on our behalf, we only need to be still.

In contrast, verses 15-17 of Psalm 135 says, "The idols of the nations are silver and gold, made by the hands of men. They have mouths, but cannot speak, eyes, but cannot see; they have ears, but cannot hear, nor is there breath in their mouths." Our God is alive and working in us and for us. He wills, he provides, and he creates and protects. And idols? They establish nothing, provide nothing, create nothing, and certainly do not protect anything. We take something we believe will provide what we are looking for and seek fulfillment from it. Yet any replacement for God, will *never* act on our behalf. We will always be chasing it; it will never be chasing us.

The problem I have found is that it is very difficult to hand over our identities, values, or purposes to something or someone we have no control over. We like to have a say over our own lives. Even if we believe we are suffering, we also believe that we have the opportunity to make it right. We have control. To just hand over control goes against our very nature, yet I believe it is what the Lord calls us to do. As long as we have a hand in our pursuit of perfection, we will never be free from it. We will always be in pursuit. However, in order to hand over something so fragile, we have to have confidence in the one we are handing it to. We wouldn't just hand something fragile to someone reckless. We need to understand just who exactly we are handing our very lives to so we can have the confidence to let them go.

Since I grew up in the church, you would think that I would have had a better understanding and willingness to do that. My parents were faithful Christians involved in church, ministry, and outreach, but more than that, they were adamant about our personal pursuit of the Lord. They would always encourage us that our personal pursuit of

Jesus would change our lives, but at the time I was still struggling with my pursuit of perfection. Even in my faith, I saw it as something I could control. I saw my salvation, my worthiness to God, as something I could achieve. My pursuit of the Lord was really about my pursuit of righteousness, and my pursuit of righteousness was really about my pursuit of perfection. I didn't have a full understanding of what a relationship with the Lord looked like. I looked at Him as someone who had the power to save me, but I had to let Him know if I was worth saving. It all depended on me. I had the control. I couldn't fully surrender to the Lord because I didn't understand who He was and how He saw me.

Honestly, I have lived most of my life this way. I have exhausted myself trying to be worthy of saving when my own reality keeps proving to me that I'm not. I constantly face my imperfections and failings so in my mind, my worth to the Lord is always fluctuating. If I am doing well spiritually: ministering, serving, and being consistent in my pursuit of God, then I am worth saving. If I am struggling, selfish, and unmotivated, then I am not worth saving. With this mindset, the pursuit of perfection is vital in my relationship with God. In fact, it means everything. If we pursue perfection, our very salvation is dependent on us and it is a heavy burden to bear.

I had no idea I was living in this pattern of faith. It wasn't until I faced an imperfection I could not fix, that I was forced to see myself through God's eyes. I had to come to Him, ready to rewrite the way I saw the Lord and, therefore, myself. I had to learn what grace was. I didn't understand it, believing salvation came through the pursuit of perfection, so grace was hardly a concept I needed.

If we don't understand grace, then we don't understand the Lord. If we don't understand the Lord, we will never understand ourselves. When we begin to see God for who He really is, we will see ourselves for who we truly are.

That's what I needed, I needed to redefine my faith. I needed to truly know who the Lord was and what He thought of me. I needed to exchange my pursuit of perfection into embracing the pursuit of grace.

Perhaps that is why I had such a battle after the affair. I didn't know what it was for God to define me, so I wasn't prepared when my own derailment happened; there wasn't a plan. I did not define myself by God to begin with, so when I felt broken, I really did not know how to define myself at all. The only definition I could come up with was based on my shortcomings. They were who I was and I spent years trying to make up for them.

It was really the story of the Israelites that opened my eyes. They were a people chosen by God to be His loved ones. He wanted to care for them, provide for them, and protect them. He wanted to define them, but Israel would not return His love. They were self-seeking, constantly in pursuit of what they believed was better, flattering Him with their tongues but rejecting Him with their actions. They wanted control over their lifestyle, how others perceived them, and the power they had. They lived lives rejecting the Lord and pursuing themselves.

Isaiah 65:1-2 says, "I revealed myself to those who did not ask for me; I was found by those who did not seek me. To a nation that did not call on my name, I said, 'Here am I, here am I.' All day long I have held out my hands to an obstinate people, who walk in ways not good, pursuing their own imaginations." The Lord was in pursuit of His people, hands stretched out, like a father behind a child just learning to walk, yet all the Israelites could do was run the other way.

Throughout the Old Testament, we see God pursue His people. He longed to dwell with them, provide for them, and strengthen them. No matter how many times they turned from Him, He was still in pursuit. Even in His anger and sadness, there was mercy and compassion. His people did not ask for Him, they did not seek Him, but He was there anyway, ready to reveal His true nature. Isaiah 30:18 says, "Yet the Lord longs to be gracious to you; he rises to show you compassion." Even in rejection, the Lord rose each morning with new mercy. Compassion was His desire.

It was in Isaiah that my heart was pierced with the character of God. Because of Israel's rejection of the Lord, He had deserted them; He could no longer live in the midst of their sins. They had made their choice and it was not Him. But God says in Isaiah 62 that in His mercy they would be given a new name. They would no longer be called "Deserted," but would be called, "Sought After." I love that. Despite their spirit towards Him, despite their rejection, He was in pursuit of them. He would inspire them with His love.

In reading their story with a heart that was broken, I began to see the Lord as the pursuer, and me as the runner. I was just like Israel, wanting control over my life, successes and failures. I wanted my perfection to define me. No matter how hard the Lord chased me, I turned my head toward fulfillment by something I could control.

Jeremiah 2:13 says, "My people have committed two sins: They have forsaken me, the spring of living water, and have dug their own cisterns that cannot hold water." We are a people constantly drawn to fulfill ourselves. It is as if we are kneeling next to a river, digging a hole beside it to find water. As foolish as that sounds, it is what we do. We are constantly looking outside of the Lord beside us for fulfillment when all we need is next to us.

It was in my broken state that I began to realize I needed to redefine myself. Even in my failings, even in my brokenness, I was the one who was pursued. I had it wrong all along. I was *never* supposed to be pursuing perfection. I was *never* supposed to be in pursuit of anything. In fact, it was in the pursuit of my own perfection that God's grace was pursuing me with His arms stretched out!

Now, with dreams that were crushed and plans that were broken, knowing I was the pursued changed everything. In fact, it meant freedom. I no longer had to be a slave to perfection; I no longer felt the need to perform. Something totally new was defining me, something more fulfilling than anything I had ever pursued, *grace*! When we choose to live in grace, we choose to be defined by it. I didn't have to keep pursuing anymore. The Lord knew that in all of my planning, in all of my dreaming, perfection was not in my reach. I could not attain it, but like a faithful father, He was there behind me, ready to catch me when I fell, knowing all along that I would. The Lord did not need me to have it all together. He did not need me to have everything right. He simply wanted me to turn around and open my arms to Him. Grace was coming for me all along—I just needed to stop running.

What, then, is the message for us? When we recognize that God is the pursuer, we should see ourselves as pursued. Despite our failings, our traumas, and our imperfections, we are pursued by the God who longs to show compassion, the God who shows new mercies every morning, the God with His arms stretched out. There is no burden there. We can find peace in the chaos because we know our perfection comes from the grace that pursues.

We need to plan for life to go in unexpected ways. We need to plan for failures. We need to plan for re-routing. They will absolutely be a part of our lives. There is no escaping, but that is okay. If we do not to get the job we wanted, if we do not end up married, or having children, or if we end up divorced, or with grown children who have difficulties, we do not have to let those define us. We do not need to spend our lives running; we do not need to chase the pain by trying to fix it. Instead, we can run into God's arms of grace, and show others the way.

Chapter Five

The Infection Spreads

My beautiful daughter was in fourth grade. I was home-schooling then and pushing for excellence in every way. I was not going to be the home school mom with the weird kids who were unsocialized and not really even educated. My children were going to be well-rounded, super-smart, outgoing children who made home-schooling look like the best option out there and, of course, make me look like the best mom ever.

But bless my sweet daughter. To her dismay, she inherited my math abilities. I didn't plan for that. Math was like a foreign language to me when I was growing up, and I desperately needed a translator. Following in my footsteps, my sweet daughter was having a hard time understanding division, and while you would think I would have empathy and compassion, my need for value came first.

One time, when she was struggling with a concept, and after multiple attempts at explaining and demonstrating it, it still wasn't making sense to her. I became frustrated with her lack of understanding and yelled, "I can't believe you don't understand this. What is wrong with you?" (I shudder typing that. How terrible.) The look on her face pierced me to my core. In two short sentences I had convinced her that my love was conditional, based on her ability to perform, and at that moment, she wasn't performing. My actions told her she was broken, she had no value. Her weakness defined her. Tears welled up in her eyes immediately, and I knew I had crushed her.

At that very moment, I realized what I had done. Her lack of understanding was indicating my lack of value as a teacher. I crushed her value to elevate mine. My own child. The infection of perfection was spreading, not just to me but to the ones I loved. I had allowed the infection of perfection to spread to my own daughter and it broke her.

Whenever we seek perfection and fulfillment outside of God, it tends to take over our lives in multiple aspects. I can only say that from experience. See, the need for the perfect image became an uncontrollable disease for me. It spread like an infection to other areas of my life and infiltrated my relationships. Every decision I made seemed to be persuaded by the value it gave me. It is heartbreaking for me to admit this, but it is the hurt I caused my daughter that finally made me aware of the damage I was doing. Not only did I chase my value through my weight, but my desire for value began spreading to those around me, starting with my children; I needed my children to give me value as well. I was not raising them for the betterment of themselves, but rather to make myself look good.

I ask for a little grace here because it was never my intention to do that. I was not even aware I was doing it, but I was. I wanted to look like a good mom with well-behaved children. I wanted them to look the part, play the part, and when they did, I had value. The problem is that every child, or person for that matter, struggles. No one is a perfect human. Children and adults have strengths and weaknesses, so when we put our value in people, whether they're our spouses, our children, or our peers, our value will always fluctuate. When they are doing well, our value increases; when they are struggling, our value decreases. What a burden to put on someone, especially a child.

In thinking about the younger generation, I've realized that the infection of perfection is spreading even outside my family. It starts in the early years and multiplies exponentially with each passing year. As parents, we want our children to do their best and be the best, because after all, they are representing our parenting. From early ages, we put them in sports, dance, music, and acting, secretly hoping they'll shine a little brighter than all the other children.

I think we can agree that when our children succeed and do well, it makes us stand a little taller, hold our heads a little higher, as if it has been all our fantastic parenting that got them where they are. I'm not saying it's necessarily a bad thing; I think we should all be proud of our sweet children in all their attempts at growth. Besides, parenting is hard work and sometimes we need a little encouragement to feel like we're doing a good job. So I'll say right now that if your child is doing great at a certain endeavor, be excited, be proud.

We must be careful not to seek our identities through our children. It becomes too heavy a burden for them. They begin to easily recognize when they are not giving their parents the value they desire. If a boy is consistently striking out in baseball and the parents seem disappointed in him during and after the game, it sends a message to him that his abilities dictate his value to his parents. If he does well, he is a success and makes them proud. If he does not do well, then he is a failure and a disappointment to his parents.

If a child is into the arts more than sports, if a student struggles in school or is not socially accepted, we can get frustrated, and through our frustration we may suggest to our children that they are not what we hoped they would be. I'm sure some of you can relate to this in your own upbringing, or in your own parenting.

The pursuit of perfection spills over into the future generations. Our pursuit of perfection will demand their pursuit of it, as well. Instead of modeling for our children that performance equals perfection and perfection equals acceptance, we should be modeling that imperfections are real and something that should bring all of us closer together.

As parents, and even just an older generation, we should be sure to show that our love is unconditional. Perfection or imperfection does not change the way we see the future generation. We can begin to give the future generation hope of living life in the freedom of grace, instead of the prison of perfection. It's time to end the cycle of performance-based living. In learning to accept grace for ourselves we can then begin to extend it to future generations and show them the way.

The more I read about depression and suicide rates climbing in young children, the more disturbed I am, as should all of us. In an article in *UCLA Health*, Sandy Cohen states, "Suicide is the second-leading cause of death among people ages 15 to 24 in the U.S. Nearly 20% of high school students report serious thoughts of suicide and 9% have made an attempt to take their lives," (Cohen, 2022).

This should be heartbreaking to all of us and should cause us to ask, "Why? What could we be doing better?" In the same article, *UCLA Health*'s Dr. Fleisher says, "For some folks, relying on other people and reaching out for help has been so difficult or seems so shameful that they just can't bring themselves to do it. So, they take on more and more, and think maybe that they need to take on more and more, to look strong for people, or to be strong. And everybody has a breaking point,"(Ibid).

We are raising a generation of humans too afraid to ask for help because they feel ashamed. Our pursuit of perfection is infiltrating the younger lives around us, and they feel they can't keep up. It is up to us as the older generation to start changing the narrative and it begins with relieving the pressure to perform in order to be loved. If we can teach them to embrace their imperfections from their younger years, maybe it won't come as much of a shock when they are made aware they have them as they get older. I'm not saying that we should expect nothing from our children so they don't feel the pressure, but I am saying that we should be clear that our love is not dependent on their ability to perform. They will be loved as imperfect people, whether they perform well, or not.

This is why we should share our testimony about the pursuit of grace. We need the future generations to understand that they are imperfect, they will make mistakes, they may not be accepted, but none of that has to define them. In fact, we need to make clear that imperfections are necessary in life. Without imperfections, we wouldn't understand or appreciate change, growth, wisdom, or perfection. Without wounds we wouldn't understand healing. It's the messiness of life that draws us toward a remedy. If there were no messiness, there would be no need for Christ. We, as a generation learning to overcome the pursuit, must show the next generation that pursuing the grace of God defines them; arms of grace are pursuing them, following behind them, waiting for when they fall, and they *will* fall. Just as we are not, they are not defined by imperfection. Their value does not come from how other people see them. Their value comes from the pursuit. They are pursued by a God who loves them despite their imperfection. He is willing to accept their broken pieces because He knows only He can put them back together. They need to learn that, as well.

I recently read an article about an ancient Japanese form of pottery called Kintsukuroi, or Kintsugi. It was really the picture that caught my eye. It was a beautiful neutral-toned pot, lined with gold cracks throughout. The two materials were integrated in a captivating way. The neutral-toned pot was nothing unusual, it was just a shiny clay pot, but the gold-filled cracks drew my eye. It was so beautifully messy, not at all something to scoff at, but something to be in awe of. In doing a little more research, I learned that the Japanese had found a way to repair broken pieces of pottery in a manner that enhanced the broken pieces and made them the focus of the art. They wanted the cracks and broken pieces to be visible. In the article, Stefano Carnazzi explains the process: "This traditional Japanese art uses a precious metal—liquid gold, liquid silver or lacquer dusted with powdered gold—to bring together the pieces of a broken pottery item and at the same time enhance the breaks. The technique consists in joining fragments and giving them a new, more refined aspect. Every repaired piece is unique, because of the randomness with which ceramics shatters and the irregular patterns formed that are enhanced with the use of metals," (Carnazzi, 2016).

This beautiful art piece was created from broken pieces of a pot, which would seemingly serve no purpose. Those broken pieces were joined together by a beautiful gold metal that would actually create a stronger pot, while at the same time making it more valuable. It was the broken and the refined pieces, and the gold, that gave the pot its true beauty and value.

This is the revelation we should be sharing with the future generation. True beauty comes from the broken pieces. It is healing that reveals true beauty and value. It is the Lord working in broken people that provides anything in our life worth displaying. The broken pieces, the messy scars, the deep wounds all cry out for someone who can love and can heal, no matter how bad those pieces, scars and wounds are. It's through the scars that we find grace, and it is grace that fills the cracks, strengthens the pot, and makes the result worth seeing. I wish I'd had that mindset with my own daughter. I wish I could have accepted my own imperfections so I could have accepted hers, so she could accept hers. I wish I had pointed to her weaknesses as something God could use to create beauty. I wish I had shown her what it means to accept the pursuit of grace.

I was awakened to this necessity of grace-based parenting by a dear mentor of mine, Helen. She's one of those moms you aspire to be like. She's humble, quiet, and has wisdom that only a life well-lived would offer. She's open and honest, yet willing to listen and understand. She'll laugh with me, cry with me, and walk through life with me and others. She's the kind of mentor every young woman or young mother should have.

In one of our many conversations, Helen began to reveal her journey as a mother and the power of God working within her. Helen's dream was to be a Christian wife and mother. She grew up in a home devoted to spiritual growth and worship and wanted to raise her own family in the same way. She was committed to teaching her children to love the Lord with all their hearts. They memorized scripture, did service projects, visited the elderly, and were at church every Sunday and Wednesday.

From her childhood years, Proverbs 22:6 was the mission —no, the command— for any parent: "Train a child in the way he should go; and when he is old, he will not depart from it." In other words, your child's perfect response to your parenting will reflect your success as a parent. Unfortunately, Helen believed the lie that perfection came from performance, so that is what she demanded. That was her goal. If her children grew to be faithful to the Lord, then she would have fulfilled her role as a Christian mother. If they were not faithful to the Lord, then she would have failed in her role. The pressure was on.

As Helen's children got older, she worked even harder to ensure that they would live their lives according to her direction, not because of her personal need for it, but rather to avoid the painful scars that a diverted or derailed life could produce. She knew well the type of wounds that caused scars and worked hard to raise her children in a way that would help avoid them.

Throughout her children's teenage years, there were typical challenges: peer pressure, lack of responsibility, lack of motivation, and the like. She met these challenges head on, confident that her faithful parenting would provide a successful outcome. When one of her children reached her teen years, something began to change. There was unprecedented behavior that grew into rebellion. There were attitudes, anger, and bitterness, which morphed into lying, sneaking out, and secrets.

The more her daughter rebelled, the tighter Helen's grip became. She could feel her daughter slipping away, and the hope of reaching her heart was slipping along with it. No matter how hard she tried, no matter how many conversations, hugs, and affirmations, it wasn't enough. Helen became filled with self-doubt, questioning whether or not she was consistent enough, hard enough, or loving enough.

What about, "Train your child in the way he should go, and when he is old, he will not depart from it"? Why were all of her efforts in parenting not working? The nights were sleepless and the days endless. The tighter she held on to her daughter, the worse it got. Scars were coming, and there was nothing she could do to stop them. Helen felt like not only was she failing her daughter, but she was failing the Lord.

Helen's aspirations in parenting are probably like most Christian mothers'. We all want to raise children who are faithful to the Lord, making decisions in their own life that would reflect the godly parenting we worked so hard to achieve. As a parent, I think it is safe to say that we pour ourselves into our children. We think about them, function around them, make decisions for them, and guide them for eighteen years and then some. We pray that everything we have done will help prevent any decisions that will cause deep regrets, wounds, and scars for their lives. We want our ideas of "perfection" to become their ideas of perfection.

We make Proverbs 22:6 our mission, so in the end our children will not depart from our teaching. If our children would just heed our advice, then so much would be avoided. I wonder if that is how our Heavenly Father feels about us. If we would just listen to His words, heed His warnings, and live out His ways, then we could avoid the scars that would come our way. But we don't. And what if our children don't? What if all of our godly parenting doesn't produce the life we want for our children?

It was years later when Helen found out that her daughter had serious bipolar disorder. Finally, the unprecedented behavior had explanations, but it didn't take the pain away, it just added to Helen's guilt. In not understanding her child, she could not effectively reach her. In her desperate attempts to rescue her daughter from a life of bad decisions and pain, she began to approach her with the intention to fix, instead of pointing to grace. Helen's daughter began interpreting her mom's behavior as frustration and embarrassment of her; there was shame and guilt. She came to believe that her parents saw her as broken; if that's how they saw her, that was what she must be.

It wasn't until her children were adults that Helen was able to come to terms with her pursuit of perfection. She realized that all through her child-rearing years she had taken upon herself too much responsibility for her daughter's spiritual success. She unintentionally had not trusted God enough to work in His way in her daughter's life to reach her heart.

In one of our many conversations, she shared with me her regret. "I always felt that I was the one who had to do all the work of parenting. I pressured myself to get everything right. My success as a mom was tied to my child's success in her faith. Perfection was what I was living for and scars from a messy life were not going to fit the mold. I wanted her to live a life unmarred by sin. It took time for me to realize that I needed to just be still and let God work on my daughter's heart. I didn't have the power God has. I had to be willing to let there be scars, the very thing I tried so hard to prevent. Through her scars she learned she needed God, and that God still loved her, even with them. The truth is, without the scars, grace can never be experienced. If we live in the pursuit of perfection, we will never understand what it means to be perfectly loved despite it."

Through Helen's words I came to realize that our imperfections are necessary if we are to experience the healing grace of Christ. I had been so deluded by the infection of perfection, that I was resistant to the remedy and instead spread the contagion.

One of my favorite stories has become the parable of the prodigal son (Luke 15:11-32). In this story a man had two sons. One son was faithful to him, obedient, and hardworking. The other son was impatient, living wildly and squandering wealth. It would have been easy in this story for the father to demand his children's obedience, and perhaps he did. It would also have been easy for him to expect their perfection, all in the name of avoiding scars, and perhaps he did. The second son ran away and continued living his self-indulgent, wasteful life, but I think the father knew something with which we struggle, as well. In seeking or demanding perfection, we miss the opportunities to experience grace, and to give it to others so it may affect them, too. We never experience a life transformed by grace because we spend so much time demanding a life we think has no need for it.

After suffering the consequences of living a life outside of God, the prodigal son, wounded and scarred, returned home, hoping for just a hint of the life he'd had before. He was a broken soul longing for grace. His father, upon seeing his son a long way out, ran to him, threw his arms around him, and kissed him. In 22-24 the father tells his servants, "Quick! Bring the best robe and put it on him. Put a ring on his finger and sandals on his feet. Bring the fattened calf and kill it. Let's have a feast and celebrate. For this son of mine was dead and is alive again; he was lost and is found." Even after his son had left, despite the bad decisions, the wounds and scars, the father was ready to complete his parenting mission. Maybe he was aware of it, maybe he wasn't, but in his response to his son, the father was teaching him something about grace. It is in the greatest moments of brokenness that grace can do its greatest healing. It comes running to bind up the wounds, conceal the scars, and breathe new life into a broken soul. That is what the father did in those moments of forgiveness. He was breathing new life into his son, teaching him that grace was there all along, despite the wounds and the scars, it was just waiting for him to turn around. Not only was the father displaying this pursuit of grace to the son who left, but he also was displaying it to the son who had been faithful and stayed. Both sons were in desperate need of a better understanding of what a pursuing grace looked like. Both sons needed to be transformed.

Perhaps that is what parenting is really about. I have to admit that I still have a way to go in my parenting journey, but as I listen to parents whose children are grown and gone, I hear one consistent theme: the need for grace. Parents need grace and children need grace. Perhaps parents are to model the way. When we choose to live in grace, we model acceptance of it to our children and to future generations. If we approach the future generations with an understanding of our own imperfections and need for grace, then perhaps we will not be so demanding of their perfection. We don't have to approach them with the goal of "fixing" them, but we can point them to the One who can make them whole, the One who can bind their wounds and heal their scars.

As Helen worked to repair the damage her parenting had done to her daughter, she began relying more on the power of God. It became less of "I" parenting and more of "God" parenting. She was committed to living a life of faith, planting seeds, and pointing her daughter to the One who could heal all wounds. She learned to admit her weaknesses as a mom, but used them to point to Christ. Where she was weak, Christ was strong. As she began to let go of her fixing mentality, she began to submit to the power of God working in her children's hearts, just as He had in hers. It could look ugly, it could get scary, there could be scars, and it could be painful, but the Lord was at work, pursuing her children. Besides, He loved them even more than she did.

Unfortunately, it took Helen's daughter a long time with a life full of bad decisions, broken promises, stress, and hurt to begin her own search for help. When she did, Helen was right there waiting for her. She drove her to every recovery meeting for two years. She listened to her pain, grief, and brokenness, but instead of trying to "fix" her, she modeled compassion and grace, not accepting the actions, but accepting the brokenness. She walked with her daughter on her journey to exemplify the unconditional love of Christ.

As I spent time listening to Helen, I realized that her journey as a parent was successful. She didn't just teach obedience to Christ, she taught the *need* for Him. In my own attempts at seeking my daughter's perfection, I had pushed out the need for Christ. I convinced her that her performance is what would deliver her.

As parents, we often teach the need for obedience but fail to teach the need for Christ. Instead, we place the burden of needing perfection on our children, We need to be testifying to our children the power of God working in broken people. They need to see it lived out in our own lives. Just as we need the grace of God to help us in our times of brokenness, so our children will need the grace of God in their times of brokenness, but none of us will ever experience the grace of God if we don't accept that being broken is necessary. We cannot heal if we are not broken.

Many times in Deuteronomy, the Lord calls for the Israelites to "remember." The Lord called them to remember what He had done for them and beyond that, to share it with their children and their children's children. They were to testify about the deliverance of the Lord to the future generations. Deuteronomy 4:9 says, "Only be careful and watch yourselves closely so that you do not forget the things your eyes have seen or let them slip from your heart as long as you live. Teach them to your children and to their children after them."

In our own revelation of grace we are called to reveal to our children our own story of deliverance. We are to help them understand what the Lord has had to teach us about self-worth and identity and apply it to them, so they can then teach it to their children. We cannot do that if we are allowing the infection of perfection to spread. It must be stopped.

As the Israelites approached the land of Canaan, the land promised to them for deliverance, the Lord reminded Israel in Deuteronomy 9:5-6, "It is not because of your righteousness or your integrity that you are going to take possession of their land. . . . Understand, then, that it is not because of your righteousness that the Lord your God is giving you this good land to possess, for you are a stiff-necked people."

Israel had done absolutely nothing deserving of deliverance. They were rebellious, stiff-necked, and unrighteous. However, Deuteronomy 7:8 says, *"But it was because the Lord loved you* and kept the oath he swore to your forefathers that he brought you out with a mighty hand and redeemed you from the life of slavery," (emphasis added.) Israel did absolutely nothing deserving of the Lord's pursuit of them. In fact, they were broken, wounded, and scarred, but it was because of the Lord's love for them that He pursued them. That is the message we should believe about ourselves, and then begin sharing with the future generations. We are loved and pursued, not because we qualify ourselves as such, but simply out of the Lord's goodness and grace.

We will never qualify ourselves for love because of our ability to perform. Love from the Lord is given freely, and that should impact the way we see ourselves and the way we see others. We do not have to expect our perfection or their perfection. It's time to change the narrative.

Chapter Six

Grace Revealed

It had been years since I'd seen my friend Erin, but there we were, sitting outside a quaint restaurant, having brunch, and finally catching up. We'd known each other since we were little—childhood friends who grew to be adult friends. Whenever we got together, it was as though no time had passed at all; there was laughter, tears, and genuine confession. Life had taken us in different directions to different states, to raise families of our own, yet we were still linked in spirit.

I'm not sure what led to such revelations that day, except they were prompted by the Lord. I believe He knew we both needed it. Through our laughter and conversation about the joys and trials of adult life, real pain began to emerge. It was ugly. Both of us had hidden the truth for so long, but it was now making its entrance, changing our lives forever.

I don't remember how the conversation took the turn it did, but I do remember her face when it began; I do remember the tears. I sat there in complete silence as my dear friend began to reveal the sexual abuse she had experienced as a child while we were such young friends. I'd been to her house, we'd had sleepovers, but the conversations never turned to that. I had no idea. Throughout her childhood, Erin was abused by someone she was supposed to be able to trust, someone who took advantage of his position. She began to reveal to me the ugly details of her past as we sat outside that restaurant. She explained with heartbreak how it had taken both a mental and a spiritual toll on her.

Over the years, Erin's suppressed traumatic experiences began to surface and produced deep anxiety, anger, insecurity, and identity issues. Anxiety reared its ugly head in a car lot one day after she was pressured to buy a car she couldn't afford. She felt betrayed and taken advantage of, a familiar, painful feeling she felt in her soul. Something so small and seemingly insignificant became a complete disaster because of the triggers of trauma. Even the smallest amount of pressure or deception would send Erin into hysterics.

Her deepest scar, however, was due to the betrayal of her trust. She didn't know who was dependable, who would deceive her, or who would take advantage of her. She approached every relationship with caution and put up barriers that seemed impossible to break down. She couldn't trust her judgment, couldn't stand up for herself, and could easily be manipulated. Everyone was dangerous; besides having no one to trust, she could not even trust herself.

My dear friend revealed that she had learned, over the years, how to keep shameful things a secret, which allowed more shameful acts to sneak in unnoticed. Abuse as a child grew into abuse as an adult. Erin confessed that while the abuse should have made her shy away from any type of intimacy, instead it did the opposite. She hated the way she felt about herself and longed to feel desirable and loved, so she gave in to relationships she knew would prove to be just as hurtful. Besides being the victim, she was also inflicting shame, guilt, and embarrassment on herself.

For twenty years, she took on the identity of how she felt... disgraceful, disgusting, and guilty. She committed herself to a life sentence of pain, which was what she felt she deserved. She somehow mustered the strength to cover it up with humor and busy-ness, portraying to those around her the picture of perfection, while on the inside she was anything but that.

After yet another traumatic relationship, Erin finally had enough. She had enough of being a sexual object, enough of seeing herself as gross and unworthy, enough of putting others' wants and needs above her own, and enough of hiding in and taking on shame that was never meant for her. That was not living, it was just slowly dying.

She was breaking and it was in that moment that the Lord began putting people in her life and putting her in places to get the healing she yearned for. He brought her to a program that would help her find her identity in the Lord, and find the courage she needed to face the past, bravely say the words, and face the people who had hurt her.

The first step to recovery was re-identifying herself. Erin had to learn to give grace to the person she had become, to put blame where it belonged, and to forgive herself for the mistakes she made because of the trauma. She knew she was a runner, she knew she was broken, and she knew she was continuing the damage. It was time to start over and seek a new identity through the grace of God.

The story of Hosea became a lifeline for her. Hosea was a prophet called by the Lord to marry an unfaithful wife in order to reveal to Israel the relationship they had with the Lord. Just as Hosea's wife, Gomer, was consistently unfaithful to her husband, so Israel was to God. Despite their poor attempts to do otherwise, the Israelites were constantly drawn elsewhere in seeking fulfillment. Hosea 4:7 says that Israel "had exchanged their glorious God for something disgraceful." That is what Israel had done since the beginning; they had constantly exchanged Him for something shameful, something that could never take His place.

Yet, despite all of Gomer's brokenness, despite her rejection of him, Hosea still pursued her. In the same way, the Lord tells Israel in Hosea 2:19, "I will betroth you to me forever, I will betroth you in righteousness and justice, in love and compassion. I will betroth you in faithfulness, and you will acknowledge the Lord." The Lord was seeking commitment from the Israelites even though they were not seeking a commitment with Him. They were longing to be fulfilled elsewhere.

Despite Israel's pursuit of her "lovers," the Lord was in pursuit of them. He was anxious to define them with his compassion and faithfulness. It was with this story that Erin began to see the pursuit of grace; that the Lord was in pursuit of her, no matter her broken life. No matter how disgusting she felt, no matter how unworthy she believed she was, the Lord was after her. She found new identity in His revealing of His grace.

In Hosea 2:23, the Lord renames Israel from, "Not my people," to "You are my people." They were a people chosen by God, a God who would seek to make them whole. Erin was the Lord's. In His pursuing grace, He came for her, bound up her wounds, made her whole, and redefined who she was.

Remember when we were little and we all ran out to recess full of excitement and relief that our brains could finally take a break? (Maybe that was just me.) For most of us, recess was the best part of the school day! It was the time to run, to play tag on the playground, and to make new friends. For me, though, recess was ruined quickly when kickball began. If you have ever played kickball, you may know exactly what I'm talking about.

To play kickball, you need teams, and what better way to pick teams than to have two captains choose their players from a group of self-conscious ten-year-olds. The anticipation of being chosen was enough to make us sick. As the last names were called, the feelings of unworthiness rapidly increased. Everyone knows that the last two people picked are the ones no one wanted. They are the people that "have" to be chosen. They are not really chosen at all; they are just the ones thrust upon the team. It's a horrible feeling if you are one of the last two chosen.

Even now, adults are receiving therapy for the insecurities that have arisen from such a situation, but with Christ, there is no "last two." We are chosen first. Every. Single. Time. There are no most favorites, and there are no least favorites. With Christ, there is no humiliation. With Christ, there is only the pride of being chosen. Remember the joy of being chosen for a team and not being one of the final two? There was a huge sense of relief, a sense of camaraderie with your teammates, and a feeling of belonging. There is something to be said for being chosen. There is a relief, an identity that takes place once your name is called, and with Christ, our names have been called.

I was recently given an article written in 2011 (Babu, 2011). It was about a group of Indian girls who were seeking a new identity. Upon their births, their parents or grandparents had named them names like, Nakusa or Nakushi, meaning "unwanted." Can you imagine? Because these girls were just that... girls, they were being discarded by their own families. They would not bring the value a boy would bring, so they labeled them with an identity they had to carry for life. Every time they wrote their names, they were writing, "unwanted." Every time they introduced themselves, they were proclaiming themselves "unwanted." This was the identity they had to carry and share with anyone they came into contact with.

Well, these strong girls decided to carry it no longer. I was smiling as I wrote this because I find their strength and determination for new identities beautiful! In braided hair, fine dresses, and with bouquets of flowers, these girls received a name-changing ceremony. They were no longer going to be called "unwanted." Instead, they chose names such as, Vaishali, meaning, "prosperous, beautiful, and good." They were made new, and I wish I could show you their picture. Every single girl is smiling from ear to ear. I wish I could just hug their necks and say an "Amen." When living in an identity that destroys you, receiving a new one does just the opposite: it brings you life, and these girls were given a new life.

Erin also found direction for change in John 4, where we witness an encounter between Jesus and someone familiar with rejection, a Samaritan woman coming to draw water from the well. She was an outcast, a woman involved in multiple relationships, coming to the well at a time when no one else would be there, no one to judge, no one to condemn. She was broken, in need of rescuing, and at this well, she encountered the grace of God. He told her in John 4:13, "Everyone who drinks this water will be thirsty again, but whoever drinks the water I give him will never thirst. Indeed, the water I give him will become in him a spring of water welling up to eternal life."

This once rejected woman was in pursuit of something that would provide temporary relief, something she would have to constantly replenish, but Jesus pursued her with something that would truly satisfy. The relief He offered would bring life, and life everlasting. Perhaps the water He provided here is the same water that was provided for Hagar so long ago when she was in her own moment of desperation. Just as with Hagar, Jesus saw the Samaritan woman, heard her, and then delivered her. Grace was in pursuit.

My favorite part about this story is in verse 28. It says that she left her water jar and went back to the town. After her encounter with the grace of God, she ran back into town to tell others of her experience with Jesus, leaving her water jar behind. She had come to the well to seek fulfillment through well water but left the very thing she came for at Jesus' feet.

It is at the moment we experience grace that our life is forever changed, and we find true fulfillment. We are no longer ashamed of needing to be seen, heard, and delivered. We are ready to run into town and tell everyone about it.

In understanding the Lord's view of the Samaritan woman, Erin began to accept the grace of Jesus and extend it to herself. She gave herself grace when remembering her past decisions, when she reacted instead of reflected, when she didn't like the way she felt or looked. She gave herself grace when she fell into the trap of fear over faith, and when she didn't live up to her own expectations. Her broken pieces were not going to define her anymore—the pursuit of grace would. She was finally starting to see herself the way the Lord saw her.

Throughout Erin's counseling, she often heard the phrase, "Hurt people, hurt people." Perhaps you have heard it, or have had to understand. It means that people who have been hurt in their own lives, who have dealt with rejection, trauma, or abuse, tend to project that hurt onto others around them. They don't know how to deal with their pain, so they act on it instead. Erin began to see that the people who had hurt her were acting out of their own hurt, and in a strange way, she could relate to her abusers. She, too, had acted out of pain and trauma in ways that were hurtful. She ran to things and people that would never satisfy. She was angry. She was defensive and untrusting. She projected her pain instead of dealing with it.

Erin had come to realize that she, too, was in desperate need of healing. She began to realize that "Healed people, heal people." If she could somehow find healing from her pain, perhaps her abusers could too. In accepting the grace the Lord had extended to her, Erin made the difficult decision to forgive and to extend grace to her abusers. By no means did she accept their sinful behavior, but she chose to see the broken person in need of healing. In realizing their brokenness, she was able to put the guilt and shame where it belonged: on their choices and their actions. They were hurt people acting out of their brokenness, undeserving, yet in need of redemption. They, too, needed Christ to heal them.

I sat in awe listening to my sweet friend's testimony of being pursued by grace. After all of the trauma she had endured, she was able to recognize God's grace extended to her, she could extend grace to herself, and then to her abusers. There was a sense of freedom in her tone. There was no longer the burden of carrying shame. She was released from the chains of imperfection and felt relief instead. My dear friend recognized Christ as the only solution to a broken world and she was ready to extend her freedom to others. She wanted to free people from the same chains that had kept her from truly living.

At the end of our conversation, she said something that brought me to tears and made me well up again, typing it. She said, "When we truly heal from our scars and no longer carry the guilt and shame of them, we then start to fully embrace our scars, share our stories, and share our hope of healing to those around us." It is difficult for many of us to imagine embracing our scars, but I believe that in order for us to move forward, in order to have any impact on those around us, we must learn what it is to be broken, and we must learn what it is to be healed. It is when true healing occurs that our desire to help others will flourish. Our scars will begin to seem less like scars and more like testimonial missions.

When serious trauma has occurred, it is easy to let it consume and define us. After all, it encompasses everything we think, feel, or do for the rest of our lives. In time, bitterness and resentment make their homes in our hearts and begin to shape the way we see ourselves and those who hurt us; we will only see them through the eyes of our pain and trauma. They are the ones who broke us, and we are the broken. It's understandable, especially when innocence was taken from us. However, Erin's testimony to the pursuit of grace reveals to us that our identity does not come from the burden of someone else's sin or hurts, it doesn't even come from our own sin or hurts.

Grace is pursuing us in the highs and lows of life. Whether we feel like the image of perfection, or we feel like the image of destruction, we are pursued. Our identities come from the undeserved love of God, not the actions of others. We need that consistency; we need that stability, otherwise our identities will always fluctuate, depending on the situation around us. If we have endured years of abuse, it will become our only identity. We must find our value and identity outside of the life we are living; we must hold tight to the only one who is consistent in his pursuit of us.

I want to make perfectly clear that just as the Lord does not accept our sinful actions, we do not have to accept the hurtful actions of others. Grace does not accept the actions of a person; it accepts the brokenness of the person. The Lord, in all His mercy and compassion, chooses to see all of us through the lens of grace, knowing full well the pain we have inflicted on Him. Hosea 11:1-4 says, "When Israel was a child, I loved him, and out of Egypt I called my son. But the more I called Israel, the further they went from me… It was I who taught Ephraim to walk, taking them by the arms; but they did not realize it was I who healed them. I led them with cords of human kindness, with ties of love; I lifted the yoke from their neck and bent down to feed them."

The grace of God tells us that despite our failings, despite our attempts to run, God is in pursuit. The Lord is seeking to save and deliver, even when we are unaware He is doing so. The more we begin to recognize that grace pursues us, even in our darkest moments, the more we will begin to realize that it is also pursuing those who caused the darkness.

I think Jesus is the Lord's grace in action. Rejection, injustice, and lies followed Christ wherever He went. Christ had every reason to abandon us to our sinful demise, yet instead He extended love. He extended His very self. This has been the pattern of God since the beginning, and I pray you are becoming attuned to it.

As we see Jesus approach His death, we see Him being constantly rejected, ridiculed, and beaten. There is every form of injustice given to Him and beyond that, absolute cruelty. There is no mercy, no compassion, and certainly no remorse from His abusers, yet in His last moments He offers this prayer, "Father, forgive them, for they do not know what they are doing."

In all the chaos, pain, and rejection, Jesus was able to see the brokenness of the people. He didn't excuse their actions by any means, but He did pursue them with grace. He understood their need for healing. This should have the most profound impact on how we view ourselves, but more importantly, on how we view those around us.

In writing this chapter, I came across an article with a story written by Corrie Ten Boom (1892-1983). You may recognize her name from the book she wrote, *The Hiding Place* (1975), in which, she writes of her experiences as a Jewish watchmaker who, with her parents and sister, assisted the underground in Holland that helped Jews get to freedom from the Nazis. The Ten Booms were discovered and put into a concentration camp. Only Corrie survived.

During one of her speaking engagements after the war, Corrie was approached by a man she knew all too well. She said this, "It was in a church in Munich that I saw him, a balding heavyset man in a gray overcoat, a brown felt hat clutched between his hands... One moment I saw the overcoat and the brown hat, the next, a blue uniform and a visored cap with its skull and crossbones. It came back with a rush: the huge room with its harsh overhead lights, the pathetic pile of dresses and shoes in the center of the floor, the shame of walking naked past this man. I could see my sister's frail form ahead of me, ribs sharp beneath the parchment of skin," (Ten Boom, 1975).

The man who had been the guard at her camp of torture was standing in front of her a couple of years later. I continued reading and Corrie spoke of how this man she had grown to despise approached her and confessed that he was a guard at the concentration camp where she and her family were held. He reached out his hand, revealed that he had found Christ, and was asking for her forgiveness. She stood there, frozen for what seemed like years, resistant to the verse that was playing in her head, "But if you do not forgive others their sins, your Father will not forgive your sins" in Matthew 6:15.

Willing herself to act, she was finally able to say the words, "I forgive you, brother, with all my heart!" (Ibid). It was these two sentences that struck my soul. She said, "For a long moment we grasped each other's hands, the former guard and the former prisoner. I had never known God's love so intensely as I did then." (Ibid).

Forgiveness in its most difficult form was the ultimate revealing of God's love. It exemplifies the pursuit of grace, even if undeserved. It is when we truly come to understand the grace of God that we begin to really understand the extent of His love.

After my conversation with my sweet friend, I went home to my closet and prayed. I felt the Lord calling me to act, to respond to this new revelation. Once revealed to Erin, she was learning to define herself and her abusers by the pursuit of grace. That was what I needed with myself. That is what I needed with my husband. For so long I had taken on the identity of his rejection and my lack of worth. Everything I thought about and did was to remedy the pain, instead of recognizing the brokenness of my husband and that "hurt people, hurt people," I took his actions as truth of who I was. He was the breaker, so I was the broken. The truth was he was broken; he needed to be healed. I was broken; I needed to be healed. We both were being pursued by grace. With us on level playing ground, I began to see my husband with eyes of forgiveness. I did not have to accept his actions or choices, but I could accept him. I could understand him as a broken person.

When we choose to live in a perfectionistic atmosphere, we not only struggle with our own imperfections, but we struggle with the imperfections of those around us. We walk around in our daily activities expecting everyone to treat us as we deserve and when they don't, we are appalled, we are offended. It is not acceptable in our world and is therefore inexcusable.

However, if we look at people through the eyes of grace, we do not have to accept their imperfect actions, but instead we can show mercy to their imperfect hearts. We can understand that they, like us, are broken people. Broken people act poorly, respond poorly, behave poorly, and show remorse poorly. It is not perfection, it is a reality that is in desperate need of grace.

With this new mindset, I began to look at my husband as an equal transgressor. He was like me, and I was like him. Perhaps understanding grace was a journey we could take together. We both needed forgiveness and a fresh start. Instead of letting his actions define or give value to me, his actions were just a revealing of his soul. My actions did not define or give value to my husband, they were just a revealing of my soul. When we made mistakes, it was because of our broken spirits. When we were doing well, it was because of our healed spirits. Either way, grace was in pursuit and changing every way we saw and dealt with each other.

As I began to see my husband through the eyes of grace, I was able to react and respond accordingly. Instead of putting up walls and having a heart full of bitterness, I broke down barriers with a heart of understanding and hope. It was as if I was giving him permission to give himself grace as well. He didn't have to see himself as the breaker and me the one he broke. He could begin to seek new definition for himself through the eyes of the Lord. Living out grace gave the chance of hope to my husband. He didn't have to live in his broken state, he too could be redefined.

I think that is why the story of David has so much more of an impact on me now than it did before. I had always struggled with David in my personal walk because we always talk about him as the "man after God's own heart." He's portrayed as a Bible hero from the time we enter cradle roll. Yet David was an adulterer. David was a schemer and a murderer. How can the two be reconciled? Would Uriah, the man he murdered, describe him as a hero? Would Bathsheba, the woman with whom he committed adultery, describe him as a man after God's heart? I do not believe so.

David's actions showed him to be anything but godly, however, because grace pursued him, his desire for a changed heart is revealed in Psalm 51. In this psalm, David had been made aware of his brokenness and realized he was desperate for healing and grace. In Psalm 51:10-12 he prayed, "Create in me a pure heart, O God, and renew a steadfast spirit within me. Do not cast me from your presence or take your Holy Spirit from me. Restore to me, the joy of your salvation and grant me a willing spirit to sustain me."

It was not the perfect actions of David that would save him; it was not his imperfect actions that condemned him. His *heart* was the true revealing of his soul, and it was changed. David was redeemed because the Lord is a pursuer, and in his pursuit forever changed the one he pursued. David was a man after God's own heart because God had been constantly after him first. Only the Lord could restore him and bring the joy of salvation. It was in recognizing his broken spirit and desperate need for God that David's heart is revealed. It was an imperfect heart that yearned for the heart of God.

I want to say I know full well that even if we pursue a life of grace towards people, it does not mean it will always be accepted or welcome. Many people are too prideful to even see their broken state, so they are unwilling to seek or accept any remedy for it. Even if that is the case, the ones who were hurt, still have the option to give grace. We do not have to accept the action, but we can extend grace, and if we do, it will still provide the healing we need. Just as Christ was willing to extend grace to an unrepentant people, it still provided healing to the world.

Looking back, I recognize the damage done in my marriage by pursuing perfection. I was always expecting and portraying the best, so

I was thrown by the worst. It did not fit the expectation of perfection. Now, learning to live in the grace of God was teaching me to never expect perfection outside of Him. Only He is perfect, and He seeks the imperfect to make us whole. My husband and I are accepting the pursuit of the Lord's grace in our broken state together, knowing full well that only He can restore and sustain us. We are broken together.

After David's prayer for a new heart, he continued his prayer in Psalm 51:13, "Then I will teach transgressors your ways, and sinners will turn back to you." David told the Lord that because of his restoring grace, David would testify to sinners about it and they, in turn, would also turn to God. David was willing to use his own sin, his own pain, to testify to others about the need for grace. There is no one better to hear that from than those who have experienced the need for it. Grace gives hope. That is why my husband and I have felt the need to speak. Our marriage is a living testament to the power and restoration of God. His pursuing grace has changed both of our lives and, in turn, our marriage. If that helps at least one life, we'll shout it.

Chapter Seven

Seeing the Broken

Remember the good old days when we used to know exactly how we'd handle any circumstance that came our way? Is that just me? When I was growing up, I remember how I would observe people living their lives, and take notes on what to do and what not to do. I became a situational expert if you will. I was so gifted that it got to where I didn't even need to know the people I was critiquing. I needed no back story, no history, nothing. I just observed and used my skills to determine what they should be doing better and how they could do it.

Finances, relationships, work ethic, you name it, I could judge it. Many a time I would listen to my parents talk about how marriage was hard work and yada, yada, yada, all the while thinking about how much I knew about being a good wife. I had been watching and criticizing wives for years. I knew what it took to make a good marriage and I knew what made a bad one. It all had to do with performance.

My expertise continued in parenting. I would watch others around me with their children, quietly critiquing and condemning their parental ignorance. Of course, I had yet to have children, but I knew when I did, exactly how I would raise them, and my sweet, obedient children would listen to my parenting wisdom and comply. It was crazy to me that others couldn't seem to get it right, but I'd show the way.

I'm hoping you caught on to my sarcasm, but I regret to say I thought my attitude was spot on. I believed I had so much wisdom to offer the world when I was younger. I chose not to understand people but rather to condemn them. I chose not to see the heart of a person, nor the broken spirit of a person. If someone was divorced, it was probably because they weren't a good enough spouse. If someone's child was living wildly, it was because the parents missed a teaching opportunity. If someone was homeless, it was because of their poor decision-making.

Everything was a result of action. In fact, in my view it was a lack of perfection that caused any chaos at all, and I was quick to point it out. I'm heartbroken at the shallowness of my spirit towards people back then. I wish I had understood more about the pursuing grace of Jesus, so that I could have extended it to those who were hurting.

My junior year of high school, I went with some friends to downtown Denver to feed the homeless. We would gather food and make blankets to distribute to the people in need, and then pray for them. It was an eye-opening and heart-wrenching experience. I will never forget a man I came across while doing this work. I don't know his name, I wish I did, but he was sitting outside next to a trashcan, warming his hands over a sewer drain. It was freezing outside.

We had one last sandwich to deliver, and he was the one person we encountered on the way back to the car. As we approached him, gave him food, and prayed over him, he noticed that I was shaking, with my hands stuffed in my pockets. He took off his gloves and gave them to me. A man who had nothing but the clothes he was wearing, warming himself by the sewage drain, took off his gloves and gave them to a girl who had plenty of clothes and had never gone hungry. I went home that night humbled. I could not believe that a homeless person would do that. That sounds terrible, doesn't it. I know. It is. I had this image of perfection that I thought everyone should live up to, and if they didn't, they were immediately judged. Instead of looking at their imperfections, I should have been looking at their precious hearts.

Kristen Lunceford

In my teen years, I remember my parents always telling me to never believe I know how to handle the situation someone else was experiencing. "If you have never experienced it," they would say, "then do not pretend you know how to handle it."

I think that probably came from their own experiences in being judged. In other words, do not look at people through the eyes of your standard of perfection, but through the eyes of grace. *See the person.* Unfortunately, it took me awhile to really understand that, and to be honest, it was my own experience of being judged that challenged me to do better.

My marital situation was exactly the type of situation that people like to give opinions and judgments on. I had been judgmental in the past, so it was only natural to have it happen to me now. People who were unaware of the details were quick to give suggestions or critiques on how to handle a broken marriage, when all I wanted was to just be seen.

I wanted someone who would sit with me in my brokenness and let me cry. I wanted someone to acknowledge that what I was going through was hard. I wanted someone to pray with me. I wanted grace. Looking back, I am so thankful that the Lord took the time to teach me to see people. I am heartsick for all of the people I could have been sitting with instead of staring at. The truth is, when we experience grace, it is easier to give it. In learning God's grace for me, I could extend it to myself, my husband, children, and others. When we choose to live in grace, we choose to define others by it.

Too often we look at people's situations and we believe we know better. Instead of seeing the person in the situation, we judge the situation. We refuse to sit with the hurting, instead, trying to fix them. We do not see ourselves on a level playing field with others, but rather elevate ourselves to a level that we can "help" others reach. I don't think I have ever witnessed this more than in the year of Covid. I know. Even the word makes us cringe.

In a time when unity was needed most, we were more divided than ever. Instead of seeing the person behind the mask, or not behind the mask, we chose to only see the mask or lack thereof. Instead of seeing the person behind the vaccine, or not behind the vaccine, we chose to only see the vaccine. We missed the whole opportunity to truly see people. People were scared, suffering, and hurting, but we couldn't see any of that because all we could focus on were our self-righteous opinions. I saw so many articles posted online by believers about why or why not we should be wearing masks, why or why not we should get the vaccine, followed by a spirit of enlightenment. There was rarely compassion for the other side, for people coming from different situations. I know that sounds harsh, and it is, but it is truthful.

We, as followers of Christ, chose to see people through our lens of perfection and held them to it. We allowed our pursuit of perfection to prevent us from seeing the soul. At times I was tempted to get caught in the pursuit. It was an easy time to get offended. It's heartbreaking to me that we let it come between friendships, outreach, and worship. If only we had chosen to understand and extend grace to those of differing opinions. If only we had seen the hurting.

When I was growing up, my grandfather would always tell the story of his trips to the doctor with my grandmother, who was dying of cancer. She had bone cancer, so every bump in the car was excruciating to her fragile body. In fact, any small amount of pressure would cause her bones to break. Because of this, my grandfather would always drive slowly, taking caution with every bump, careful not to add any extra pain to his dying wife. As you can imagine, they received all kinds of hateful words, actions, and honks from passersby because of it.

As another car would pass by in annoyance, my grandfather would look at his beautiful wife next to him and wonder what the driver would do if they knew his precious wife was dying. If they could see the person who was breaking apart inside that car, would their actions and their assumptions be different? For those pursuing perfection, compassion is not easy to give. In our self-righteous spirits, it is difficult to see anyone but ourselves, it is not in our nature.

This is not just a current battle, it's one that has been around since the times of the Israelites and probably before. In Ezekiel 34 the Lord condemns the leaders of Israel, the ones who should have known better, for not seeing the hurting. It says in verses 3-4, "You eat the curds, clothe yourselves with the wool and slaughter the choice animals, but you do not take care of the flock. You have not strengthened the weak or healed the sick or bound up the injured. You have not brought back the strays or searched for the lost." They were so busy taking care of themselves, pursuing their wants and needs, that they failed to see the hurting around them! As shameful as that is, we do that. I've done that.

A few years ago, the Lord brought a woman into my life who opened my eyes more to this reality. Sarah is a beautiful friend of mine I met when she came to visit our congregation. She is quiet, filled with compassion, and seeks genuine conversation. I met Sarah around the same time I had my life-changing conversation with Erin. Through Erin, the Lord was revealing to me His desire for extending grace, even to those who have hurt us. Through Sarah, the Lord was revealing the need to see the people who were desperate for it. The Lord was pursuing me, opening my eyes to the grace-filled life to which He was calling me. I was surrounded by the power of God working in people.

After a few short conversations with Sarah, I quickly found out that her husband had left her for a younger woman. Why, I couldn't understand. She was beautiful, authentic, and adventurous. In listening to her story, I automatically felt a connection with her. She was someone who understood the pain of rejection. We started going out to dinner, going on hikes, and attempting to play tennis. Throughout our time together, we realized how much we had in common. We both struggled with our pursuit of perfection and displaying the perfect life to others around us. We both had been rejected, and we both struggled with eating disorders because of it. We were broken together.

Over time, I learned that this was not the first time she had been left by a husband. This was the second time. Both men were sons of elders in the church and leaders in the congregation, but both ended up leaving her for someone else. Now, the old me would have placed judgment on her right away. I would have made some kind of assumption that she had issues in being a good wife. She probably wasn't servant-hearted, most likely was lazy, or yelled a lot, or something like that. Again, how terrible. But because of my own situation, recognizing my own need for grace and empathy, I looked at her with compassion. I wanted to just see her as she was, in her brokenness. I wanted to sit with her in it, and perhaps she could even sit with me in mine.

Over time, we shared some of the most spiritually encouraging talks I've ever had. She helped me to see a side of the Lord I had never seen. She was gracious, humble, life-giving in speech, and compassionate to those in pain. She was a seeker of wisdom and sought the Lord's direction in everything. I was in awe and inspired by her. I realized that her trauma and tragedy made her the perfect friend for someone who was hurting, like me. She saw people just as they were, with no judgment, but rather filled with grace. After eleven years of silence, I was soon sharing my story and my pain with Sarah. There was compassion in her spirit, a genuine tone in her voice, and a life-giving grace that I desperately needed. She needed no perfection from me. She gave me no judgment. She simply sat with me, cried with me, and prayed with me.

It's heartbreaking to say this, but my life-giving, grace-filled friend was also an outcast. Her story didn't fit the mold that's wanted in the church. Sarah often sat in the back corner, not having many people to talk to, because once people found out about the divorces, they didn't dig much deeper. Yet, she was gracious. She understood. She had once been that way herself. She, like me, used to look at people with condescending eyes and a judgmental spirit, not intentionally, but just as our perfectionistic nature came out. Like I said, we like things clean and simple. We don't know how to deal with anything different.

Throughout our times together, I often listened to her cry as she talked about not knowing what her place was at church. She didn't believe she had much to offer, but with her past, probably no one would want to listen anyway. There were many nights after our meetings when I would just go home and cry out to the Lord. Knowing how beautiful a person and what a faithful example she was, I was heartbroken that she didn't feel like she had a place. She had so much to offer the church. She had been tested and tried and stayed faithful to the Lord, even when most would have given up. I realized that I felt her pain so much because I *was* her. I had spent eleven years afraid to reveal any truth about myself, living in fear of what others might think. My story was imperfect and did not fit the mold. Sarah's story confirmed to me what I felt people might do if I were to reveal my husband's and my story. We, too, would be sitting in the back corner.

I will always praise the Lord for my friend Sarah because she helped to open my eyes to people who are hurting. After I began my friendship with her, I didn't want to just come to worship, fill the pew, sing my songs, and leave, I wanted to uplift. I wanted to seek out the outcasts. I wanted to sit right next to them and become their friends. I wanted them in my home. I did not want one person to feel the way my friend Sarah had. In reality, she was the one we should have been listening to, the one who could testify to the power of God working in broken people, but we pushed her to the side, refusing to witness it.

I felt sick because I had done that very thing in my own life. I had made judgments about people because of the situation they were in, or the sin they were struggling with, and I had retreated from them. It is hard for us in the church to break down barriers. It is difficult to be genuine and dig deep into the lives of the hurting. We get uncomfortable and we don't know what to say. If we do say something, it usually comes out awkward and causes us to never speak out again. Sometimes, all we need to do is just sit with them instead of retreat from them.

The story of Job always reminds me of what living in grace should be or should not be in this case. Job was a righteous man, broken and brought low by the work of Satan. In the midst of him losing his home, his children, his flocks and herds, and even his own health, his friends came to comfort him. They started off doing great. It says in Job 2:13, "Then they sat on the ground with him for seven days and seven nights. No one said a word to him because they saw how great his suffering was." What a great way to show sympathy, to just sit with someone in their pain. No judgments, no criticism or advice, but just sitting with them.

They did so well for those seven days, but unfortunately on the eighth day, they decided to open their mouths. Their words were full of judgment, accusation, and assumption. There was absolutely no grace. This is something that we in the church should consider. When people are hurting, the best thing we can do is to see them, pray over them, and let them know we are there. The worst things we can do would be to judge them, leave them, or forget about them.

A surefire way to see if we are living in the grace of God is to ask ourselves whether we are good at giving it. Can we have compassion for those with ugly, messy stories? Can we engage with them, not just once, but multiple times, offering hope and restoration? Are we looking around us when we sit in the pews at church, intentionally looking for the people who may not fit in? My story, Sarah's story, and all the others I have shared in this book are also the stories of people sitting right next to us in church. All we have to do is get out of our comfort zones and reach out. We have to engage, we have to dig deep, and more than anything, we have to give grace. We are missing out on witnessing the power of God at work when we fail to engage in the lives of others.

Several years ago, my husband and I lost a good friend to suicide. He was a Christian, but he was struggling, struggling with sin and with finding his place. He didn't know where he fit, so he just didn't. It breaks my heart to think that he was battling alone. I wish so badly that we had done more, said more, and just sat with him more. For so long I had let the infection of perfection affect the way I saw and dealt with broken people. I did not know what to do with broken people because I had yet to see myself as broken. If only we could sit with him now after being made aware, we could all sit, broken together, ready to embrace grace's pursuit. When we are not living in the grace of God, we do not give the grace of God. When we seek our own perfection, we seek the perfection of others. We do not see the hurts of people, we see their less-thans and define them by it.

Since losing our friend to suicide, the Lord has constantly revealed this problem in my life and in the church. He brought people to me with stories of trauma, abuse, and addiction, mostly from Christian people. The underlying theme was the same: Because they had been broken, they didn't feel like they had a place in the church. Their experiences would make other people cringe, so they felt trapped by the need to keep it all in. They had to pursue the grace of God on their own, with no support from those around them. I am so thankful for those experiences and conversations because they helped me to open my own eyes to the judgmental spirit I had. Instead of isolating myself from people who were struggling or different, I should have been digging deeper, intentionally seeking them out and making sure they knew they had a place right next to me in the pew. That's living in grace.

We see the way Jesus dealt with the broken in John 8:1-11. While He was teaching in the temple, the Pharisees brought a woman to Jesus who had just been caught in the act of adultery. It is not hard to imagine the drama that must have ensued. She was most likely improperly dressed, having been caught in the act, and was then forced to stand before the group in complete vulnerability. Being rushed to where Jesus was, she was probably resisting their attempts to restrain her out of fear of the impending death that was, by law, supposed to happen. It is not a pretty picture. In fact, it is embarrassing, sinful, and dramatic.

Instead of withdrawing from her, instead of following the law of death, instead of rejecting her, Jesus pursued her with grace. He recognized her sinful nature, put her on level ground with all the "righteous people" around her, and chose unconditional love. In this moment, when everyone else was looking down on her with an air of self-righteousness, Jesus knelt down to lift her up. He was seeing the broken and provided her hope. Inspired by grace, she was called to live a different life.

At the end of the passage in Ezekiel, the Lord provides the remedy to the leader's lack of action in chapter 34, verse 16. Since the leaders would not seek out the hurting, the Lord says, "I will search for the lost and bring back the strays. I will bind up the injured and strengthen the weak." God was ready to do what others would not. It is in Jesus that he fulfilled that very mission. He was intentional in seeking out the hurting. He was intentional in lifting others up. When so many others failed to see the soul, Jesus saw.

Perhaps if we learned to dig a little deeper, to show a little more compassion, and to love like Jesus, we could provide hope to the hurting. If we remembered our undeserving life of grace, perhaps we would be more willing to give it. Luke 7:47 says, "He who has been forgiven little, loves little." If we are so quick to point out the faults in others, our faults will also come to light. Experiencing the grace of Jesus calls us all to different living. It calls us to look at people through the eyes of compassion instead of judgment. We will look for ways to heal hearts instead of condemning them.

I remember when I was in middle school and my family had gone out to eat at one of our favorite Mexican restaurants. When our waitress arrived at the table, it was clear she was not in a cheerful mood. She was cold and indifferent. My parents have never been ones to give in to their frustration with indifferent people, so they continued in their cheerful dispositions, asking her questions and trying to lift her spirits.

On one of her many trips to our table, our waitress tripped, drinks in hand, spilling them all over the floor. She immediately dropped to her knees and started to cry. My mom, in her genuine compassion, reached out to provide her some type of assurance. Upon receiving my mom's compassion, the waitress then laid her head in my mom's lap and sobbed as she described having to take care of her ailing mother. Her soul was aching. She needed to be seen. I will always look back on that event and think about the pursuit of grace my parents displayed that night. They were not thrown by her rude disposition, but rather pursued her in love. Sometimes, people just need to be seen, and when we are so focused on their actions, we miss seeing their aching soul.

I am thankful for my relationship with Sarah, who helped to open my eyes to people who are hurting. I am so thankful to have witnessed the grace of God working in her so that I could open my eyes to others who also needed His grace. Because of our conversations, I began trying to see the heart of the person, instead of their actions. Instead of judging the man on the street holding a sign, the teenage mother, the divorcee, or the rebellious child, I began to look at their hearts. I began to see the person, not the mess.

I began to wonder what their stories were, what their home life was like, and how I could reveal to them God's grace that was running after them. Imagine the world we could create if we all lived with the pursuit of grace as our mission.

Those few years I shared with my friend Sarah opened my heart to sharing my story. It is because of her that bravery began its work in me. I did not want to be seen as a mom and a wife who had it all together. I wanted to be seen as broken. I wanted to be seen as healed. I wanted to be seen as redeemed. That was the freedom I had been seeking so long: to be my broken self, to end my pursuit of the perfectionistic lifestyle, and to accept and embrace the pursuit of grace.

There are so many broken people with heartbreaking stories, and those are the people we should be living out the great commission with. We can testify to the healing grace of God, but we have to be willing to break down the walls, step off of the pedestals, and dig deep into people.

When our eyes are opened to grace, it changes the way we see others around us. We don't see them as outcasts or someone to retreat from, but rather, as opportunities to show the love of Christ. Let us allow our eyes to be opened so that we might see the beautiful souls who are broken just like us. May we get down on our knees so we can lift them up.

Chapter Eight

The Other Side of the Wall

Freedom. It's something we all crave, yet rarely attain. The daily grind of life and the pressures from everything and everyone around us are enough to make freedom seem like a perpetually distant, out-of-reach dream. It's cruel really. We are imprisoned by the cycle of constantly having to satisfy; everything we do is based on our ability to perform. If that isn't hard enough, we are then judged based on that ability. Our jobs, our marriages, our parenting everything is an opportunity, or rather, a demand, to prove ourselves, but we rarely do. It's hard not to feel enslaved to the life we have created for ourselves and that's exactly what Satan wants us to be: slaves to a life of constantly proving our worth. That is something we can never achieve, nor did God ever intend us to. Satan thrives on our hopelessness. We're living a life sentence and he enjoys imprisoning us or trying to.

It is hard to break free from the chains of bondage, especially when we've been chained for so long. We don't know what life outside of the prison walls looks like, and honestly, there's a little fear there. We've grown comfortable or at least accustomed to the life we have been living, so living outside of that reality seems intimidating. It's foreign. If only we could peek outside the walls and get a glimpse of what real freedom looks like, maybe it would be easier to step into it. The problem is that in order to break the chains of bondage, we must be willing to surrender our fear of what's on the other side, but that involves giving up control. It involves giving up the very thing that has held us captive for so long, and as easy as it seems it should be, it is not. The pursuit of perfection has been the driving force behind why we live life the way we do. If we take that away, then what life do we have? What are we living for?

I believe this must have been the way the Israelites felt after being held captive by Babylon for so long. After so many years of captivity, freedom must have been an intimidating venture. We see in Nehemiah that so many of them had grown accustomed to their new life in a foreign land, and when they were called to leave it to rebuild their own homeland, that call was met with uncertainty and fear. Now they were being called to leave their place of bondage for what seemed like another place of bondage. They would have no protection, no place of worship, and no housing. It would be a life of complete rebuilding. There would be ridicule, there would be intense opposition, and there would be heartbreak. Life on the other side of the wall didn't seem like freedom.

For most of us, surrender doesn't feel like the way to freedom. It feels like the way to enslavement. When we think of war and the men who have had to surrender, we attribute it to failure, to a battle lost. There was no more hope; the enemy had won. In fact, surrender often brought about imprisonment, torture, or death. It certainly was not the path to life. Perhaps that's why we fight so hard against it. When battle ensues, self-preservation tactics come out in full force.

However, in Christ, everything is flipped. It is in the moments of surrender that we can achieve victory. Why? Because He already fought the battle. He already won. We just have to be willing to lay down our weapons and end the fight. When we finally raise the white flag and accept the fact that we are no longer in control, the battle can be won. It's a call to do the very opposite of what our nature tells us to do, and I think that was God's intent. He wanted us to do the very thing that goes against our nature, end our quest for self-preservation, and choose Him. Choosing Him means we are no longer choosing ourselves. We are giving up the life we want for the life we are called to live and that is one of the most difficult things we could ever do. The Lord knew that it was only through a surrendering of our will that true freedom, true deliverance could come.

In recognizing the infection of perfection that had taken over my life, I recognized a serious need for change. I was in bondage to a life that only left me broken and needy. Somehow, I had to break the chains of perfection and embrace the freedom that was calling me. Somehow, I had to rebuild. The problem was that the path to freedom did not feel like the path to freedom. I was so used to my captive life that I could not recognize freedom for what it is: Freedom comes from giving up control; freedom is resting in the power of God instead of depending on myself, and freedom comes from surrender.

Because Satan loves to see us imprisoned, he comes at us the hardest when we are trying to seek a life outside the prison walls. As we are pursuing a life of freedom, he is chasing us, ready to lock the chains. Satan does not want us to rebuild. He does not want us to live with hope, and he certainly does not want us to live in freedom.

We see in Nehemiah 4 that some of the Israelites were able to push past their fears and make their way back to Jerusalem. They were anxious to begin rebuilding, however, as soon as the process began, they were met with opposition. A man named Sanballat and his friend Tobiah became angry at their attempts to start over and ridiculed the Jews as they set to their difficult task of rebuilding. Sanballat jests in chapter 4 verse 2, "What are those feeble Jews doing? Will they restore their wall? Will they offer sacrifices? Will they finish in a day? *Can they bring the stones back to life from those heaps of rubble—burned as they are?*" (emphasis added)

These enemies of Israel wanted them to believe they had no power to recover. They wanted them to believe there was no hope of being restored; there was no life on the other side of the wall. This is the same opposition we receive from Satan when we set off to rebuild. It seems that as soon as we begin our journey to recovery, he is right there along with us doing everything in his power to keep us from experiencing hope and freedom. He wants us to feel defeated because in our feelings of defeat, the power of God is muted and His message of hope to the world is muted.

As opposition to the Israelites increased, Nehemiah held true to his focus and mission: freedom; the freedom to rebuild life kept Nehemiah going. In moments of despair, his focus was on allowing the power of God to see him through. It was the Lord who would be his source of strength. He says in Nehemiah 6:9, "They were all trying to frighten us thinking, 'Their hands will get too weak for the work, and it will not be completed.' But I prayed, 'Now strengthen my hands.'" When the quest for freedom was too much to bear, Nehemiah cried out to the Lord, surrendering his strength to the One who could help him endure. I love that: "Strengthen my hands."

When seeking a life of freedom, it is inevitable that Satan will attack us on all sides. It is critical to keep our eyes focused on the True Deliverer and surrender to His path of deliverance. In moments of opposition, it is too easy to fight back for control and continue in the patterns we have been living. Rebuilding is too intimidating. To seek true freedom, we must be willing to surrender control. We must be willing to give up the comfortable and embrace the uncomfortable.

Nehemiah was able to do that because he knew who the Lord was and what He could do. The Lord was his source of strength. Perhaps we could say the same prayer as Nehemiah when faced with our own opposition, "Now strengthen my hands." As we feel the intimidation of a captive life, may our hands be strengthened so that they might let go of the chains and cling to the One who has freed us from them. May we trust that God's path to deliverance will provide just that.

When I was growing up, there was a man in our congregation named Jesse Yarborough who had fought in World War II. My family would visit him and his beautiful wife, Tina, in their home and listen to their stories of love and war. Jesse had met Tina as he was battling his way through Italy. It was obvious to everyone around them that their love ran deep. Listening to their stories was better than watching anything the movies could produce; however, one story Jesse told has stood out to me more than any other.

Jesse had been fighting his way up through Italy when he came across an enemy soldier hiding in a basement. As he was not allowed to take the prisoner with him, Jesse's commander told him to stay and wait with his prisoner until approaching troops could arrive to relieve him of his duty. Jesse waited. One day, one night, another day, and another night, but on this second night, Jesse fell asleep. Upon waking up the next day, he realized the vulnerable position he had put himself in. His gun was on the ground next to the German soldier he had captured who was staring at him. Through fumbled communication, Jesse asked the soldier why he had not killed him in the night. Why did he not escape?

The soldier replied with a smile, "Why would I do that? For me, the war is over. I get to go to America! You are the one I feel sorry for. You have to stay here and keep fighting!"

This soldier knew that it was only through surrender that a chance would come for him to rebuild. How could surrender come so easily to one who had spent so long fighting against it? Now, thinking back to World War II, would the soldier's response have been the same if the Russians had captured him? Most likely not. Why? Because the Russians were not of the same reputation as the Americans. The Americans had the reputation of gentlemen back then, but the Russians did not. The German soldier was well aware of who had captured him, so in recognizing that it made his surrender all the more natural. The soldier had no need to fight any longer; he just needed to trust that surrender was the way to freedom. Perhaps that is the key for all of us.

If you know who you are surrendering to and what your life will look like afterwards, then you will raise the white flag with minimal resistance. We will see that the glory of the other side will far outweigh the struggle to get there. We will not see surrender as defeat or as a loss, but rather as the true path to freedom, but we must be willing to give up the fight. We must be willing to put down our weapons and surrender our control.

This is where I was in my life. I was entrapped. I had been damaged, I had damaged others, and I was enslaved to a life that was breaking me. My hope of freedom was slowly fading. My marriage was suffering, my children were suffering, and others around me were suffering. The pursuit of perfection had its grip on me and had no intention of ever letting me go. It was I who had to surrender. It was I who had to let go. It was time to leave my life of captivity and rebuild. I had spent eleven years behind a wall of smiles, eleven years of portraying "perfection," and eleven years hiding that I was ever broken. After eleven years of silence, I had no choice but to seek deliverance and to seek it in the most uncomfortable way.

The room was in a converted trailer with a yellow exterior and a musty, dated interior. As I opened the door, I saw a large circle of chairs set up around the edges of the room. Women were scattered throughout thumbing through books and pamphlets; quiet conversations filled the room. I knew no one, I just knew I needed help, so I sat down in the chair closest to the door, but really, closest to the exit, just in case I needed a quick escape.

As I sat there, looking down, trying not to draw attention to myself, a woman approached me and with no hesitation said, "Hello! My name is… and I'm a recovering…" I was in shock. Never in my life had anyone ever approached me with their name and lifelong battle! She quickly went into detail about her journey and what led to her attendance at these meetings. It was too much information for me to digest. How could someone in one breath, without even a wince, and with no reservation, reveal their deepest wounds and battles? Several other women began to approach me and do the same: "Hello! My name is… and I am a recovering…" Obviously, these women had no boundaries. To say I was uncomfortable would hardly scratch the surface. They were completely vulnerable, totally open, and had no regard for the look of horror and embarrassment on my face. These women were the complete opposite of me. I did not know what to say or how to respond, and I wondered if I had made the right choice by entering that room. For years I had kept my battles a secret, and the thought of having to reveal it to women I didn't know was terrifying.

Soon after the meeting started, everyone began to go around the room and share their struggles. There were some tears, there was some heartbreak, but most surprisingly, there was pride. I know it sounds funny to say that, and it was uncomfortable to witness, but it is true. These women were proud of the power of God working in them, even if it was through their hurts, trauma, or sin. They were able to boast in their weakness because they knew their healing would provide hope and they were overjoyed to offer it! As the night went on, I found myself drawn to these women. I craved their sense of freedom. I was envious of their vulnerability. as each of them revealed her story, I felt the weight being lifted off me.

Realizing that other people had stories that were ugly, shocking, and embarrassing made me feel right at home. Perhaps I could be real. Perhaps they wouldn't judge. Perhaps I could finally be set free. My hands were shaking, my whole body was trembling as the time came for me to speak. I felt every ounce of resistance in my soul. Only by the strength of the Lord was I finally able to say, "Hello, my name is Kristen Lunceford and I struggle with pursuing perfection. I have been crushed by an affair and have spent years pursuing whatever could fill the void." Now it was real. Now I could never go back. Saying the words out loud made everything official. Finally I could move past the trauma and acknowledge my pain. I could see my choices for what they were. I could finally seek healing.

That night, I came to the realization that while many of our stories were different, they all had a common theme: broken people needing to be made whole. At one point in all of our lives, we fell captive to the enemy: the pursuit of perfection. In our brokenness we all sought healing through things or people that would never provide healing. We all needed rebuilding. We all needed to encounter the pursuing grace of God.

When I got in my car that night, I broke down. I had overwhelming feelings of embarrassment and awkwardness, but also relief. As I drove away from the meeting, I couldn't help but wonder if that was the way the church was intended to be. I wondered if the original design was for broken people to come together, telling their stories of redemption and praising the Lord who gave it to them. It felt real. It felt genuine. There was no pretense, there was no pride. No one was better than another, no problem was worse; we all stood side by side at the foot of the cross. We were all broken, we all knew it, and we were all desperate for healing. I was humbled, ashamed, and scared to go back—yet I couldn't stay away.

As strange as it sounds, getting help is one of the hardest things we can ever do. It takes a level of humility that often comes from being destroyed or from being a destroyer, which means that serious damage has had to take place in order for us to get this low. It's embarrassing. Getting help also means that we have to work, and when we're already exhausted from pursuing an unsatisfying life, any extra effort seems daunting. No one likes to feel like they have to pour more of themselves into something when they already feel emptied, but if we desire any change of outcome, we must be willing to change whatever affects it. Nothing in our lives will ever change if we do not change. We must be willing to be rebuilt.

The story of Naaman is one that so many of us relate to. Naaman was a victorious soldier by the Lord's hand; however, he also had leprosy. Leprosy was a disease that ostracized its victims from their people as it was highly contagious, extremely painful, and fatal. In searching for a cure, Naaman was introduced to Elisha, the prophet of God. Elisha gave a quick remedy and called Naaman to dip seven times in the Jordan River to receive renewed flesh.

But Naaman was not a fan of Elisha's remedy. The Jordan was dirty, ugly, and inconvenient. Naaman was desperate for healing, but not desperate enough for seven dips in the nasty Jordan. How many of us are like that in our own lives? We all want healing, but when we are called to do something we perceive as difficult and uncomfortable, the desperation seems to lessen. The truth is, we want a quick fix. We do not want to make any effort more than necessary, however, with this spirit, we cannot find true deliverance. We cannot be healed if we do not seek healing in the Lord's way. When our idea of healing does not match up with the Lord's, are we willing to choose His will over ours?

I would like to say that I quickly made the transitions I needed throughout my group counseling and began rebuilding the life God intended for me, but it took me quite a while. It was extremely difficult to break down my walls and be authentic. Even in my group's openness, I was afraid I might be judged, worrying maybe they wouldn't understand. I found myself being somewhat open, but still shading it to make sure I didn't look too bad—honest, but not vulnerable. I held back. It is terrifying to open yourself up to people and possible judgment. I wanted healing, but I, like Naaman, wanted it on my terms.

After months of slowly opening up, group members called me out on what my true struggle was. They were able to see it in me because they had once experienced the same obstacle: surrender. That became my word of the year that year. Surrender. I finally realized, after eleven years, that I struggled to give my rejection to the Lord. I allowed it to define me. I wanted to hold onto it. I wanted to remedy it myself. I wanted to control it. I wanted to prove it wrong.

Yet in my desperate attempts at control, the Lord could not do His best work in me because I had not yet fully surrendered. I needed to put the pride of His power working in me over the shame I had for needing to be worked on. I had to humble myself, take down the walls of pretense, and admit that I was broken.

In 2 Kings 5:13, Naaman's servant calls him out on his lack of surrender. He said, "My father, if the prophet had told you to do some great thing, would you not have done it? How much more, then, when he tells you, 'Wash and be cleansed'!" If Elisha's call to healing matched Naaman's own, he would have accepted it, but because Elisha asked him to do something different, he rejected it. He was being called to surrender his will, his pride, and his brokenness.

The call to surrender is really a call to let go. We must completely release the grip on our quest for control and seek deliverance in a way that is absolutely against our nature. We must give ourselves up to save ourselves. In verse 14 we see Naaman accept the proposition and cleanse himself in the Jordan. He surrendered himself to save himself. When we ask for deliverance, may we also ask for the strength to do what it takes to be delivered.

It is through the life of Christ that I had begun to wonder what my life would look like if I was willing to surrender just as Naaman had. If I was willing to give up the things I believed brought me life and deliverance, what would life be on the other side? The life I had been living until then had certainly not provided the deliverance I had been looking for; it had done nothing but hold me captive and surround me with hopelessness. What would happen if I laid my resistant spirit at His feet and surrendered to His ultimate plan for humanity?

We see the ultimate example of surrender in Christ before His journey to the cross. It is as if He is modeling for us the way to true freedom. In Matthew 26:36-46 we read of Jesus' experience in the garden of Gethsemane. His betrayer was approaching, His torture was looming, and His death was imminent. Instead of fighting back and seeking self-preservation, He was called to surrender. We see His agony in verse 38 when He tells his disciples, "My soul is overwhelmed with sorrow to the point of death… "

In Luke, we see that terror of a life called to surrender when Jesus was sweating drops of blood as He prayed in the garden. Surrender was not going to come without sacrifice; it was going to be horrific. Multiple times in the garden that night, Jesus asked the Lord to take away this calling from Him. It is difficult to view surrender as a win when you know so much pain and trauma will come from it. Jesus knew full well that the path to deliverance would eternally deliver, no matter how difficult the path would be. A life surrendered would bring freedom. It is here in the garden that one of the greatest battles was won. Victory was coming, and it was coming through the surrendered spirit of Christ. In seeking a surrendered life, we must understand that pain may be involved. It's the tearing down of something old and building up of something new. It involves pain, sweat, and tears, but the end result is a beautiful new creation.

Think of how a diamond forms. Diamonds are created from carbon atoms deep below the surface of the earth's crust. Under high temperature and high pressure, these carbon atoms begin to come together, eventually forming crystals that we call diamonds. It is the intense heat and pressure that create something so beautiful and valuable. Without those elements, beauty cannot be created. In the same way, for us to be formed into something beautiful and valuable, we must be willing to be transformed, no matter how difficult the process.

After Jesus was tortured, beaten, and nailed to the cross, He uttered His very last words, "It is finished." I do not believe He was just talking about His journey to death. He was talking about the victory and freedom He brought through His surrender. Ultimate freedom had arrived. To those on the outside looking in, it must have looked like ultimate defeat. His enemies rejoiced, the world lost hope, and His disciples were confused. Death did not look like victory. It looked like defeat. This is why so many of us resist surrender. It does not feel like victory. It feels hopeless, but it was because of surrender that Christ won. It was because of surrender that grace could make its entrance. Death was conquered, the quest for perfection was conquered, and our imperfections are now covered. It was in the moments of hopelessness that grace came running to set the captives free.

Unfortunately, I lived most of my early life as if I had not been rescued. Many of us do. For so long, I had lived in the pursuit of seeking rescue and deliverance, when it had already been provided. My call is the same call Christ had and it is to surrender to God's designed plan for us. For many of us, it means giving up what we believe has given us life for so long, when really it has imprisoned us. We are blinded by the hope we believe it provides. We see this in the story of the wealthy man in Matthew 19. He came to Jesus claiming his perfection in keeping the law, but the one thing he had yet to do was surrender. He was called to surrender the very thing he believed brought him life, his wealth. Upon receiving the call, the man went away sad. We don't know what the man's final decision was. I pray it was to lay his possessions at the feet of Jesus, but it seems from the text that he might not have done so. It might have been too difficult for him to let go. I could relate to that. Everything inside of me fought against surrender. In fact, every part of me fought for control, the very opposite of surrender.

Early one morning, after one of my recovery meetings, I sat outside on my favorite swing and I prayed for deliverance. I cried. Sobbed. Shook. I admitted to God that I had held back my pain from Him. I admitted that I had depended on things and other people to fill me when I felt empty. I admitted that I had wanted to fix myself instead of letting Him work in me. I confessed that I had transferred my need for perfection to my children and others around me. I admitted my pride, my self-righteousness, my judgmental spirit, and my lack of seeing others. I admitted to the Lord that I was terrified to rebuild, that I didn't even know what life was like on the other side of all my "walls." I asked Him to strengthen my hands so I could let go. I came to Him in pieces, broken, and desperately needing Him to make me whole. White flag.

Surrender began on the swing that day. After my confessions, I quickly went to my bathroom, picked up my scale and got rid of it. I deleted all shopping apps from my phone and dedicated myself to seeking the Lord and digging deep roots. Though fear was absolutely present and would often rear its ugly head, the more time I spent with Jesus, the more it began to decrease. The more I set my foundation on Him, the easier it was to rebuild. This time, my life was built on the way the Lord saw me. This time, my mission was built on God's design. This time, my foundation was set on grace.

That's where Peter came in. During that life-changing year, one of my favorite stories in the Bible was hardly a story at all. There is nothing to it, yet there is everything. It is something the Lord knew I needed to read, think about, and internalize. Peter was one of Jesus' first disciples in His ministry. He left his home, travelled with Jesus, witnessed His miracles, and aided Him for three years. He was zealous. He was passionate. He was ready to fight, ready to defend, and eager to act.

When Jesus was arrested and facing death, Peter was called to reveal his true identity, one defined by Christ. He couldn't. Fear kept him holding on to the safer identity, the one he could control, the one he thought wouldn't bring pain. Jesus looked Peter in the eye and Peter made the exchange: self-preservation over surrender.

In rejecting his identity with Christ, Peter lost his real identity. There was no fulfilling life outside of Christ. As the Lord approached His death, Peter witnessed the complete opposite of self-preservation; he witnessed perfect surrender. There was no protecting Himself. There was no defending Himself. He simply gave Himself up. It was the exact opposite of what Peter had done. Peter had to be feeling ultimate shame. He had to wonder if he still had a place with the other ten disciples. How could he possibly point others to Christ when he had battled so hard to avoid surrendering to Him?

We see in 1 Corinthians 15:5 that after His resurrection, Jesus appeared to Peter privately. It says that Christ was raised on the third day and then, "He appeared to Peter, and then to the twelve."

That's it. That's the story that gets me every time: Jesus appeared to Peter. I know it may seem odd, but if you put it in perspective, it's beautiful. When Peter was completely broken, without purpose, without friends, and living in shame, Jesus appeared to him. Why? Why Peter? All of the disciples deserted Him in the garden. Why did Jesus meet privately with Peter?

I know it is all speculation, but if I put myself in Peter's shoes, I believe I know why. Peter was defining himself by his brokenness, by his guilt and shame, but the Lord wanted to pursue him with grace. I know the verse doesn't say what was said in that meeting, but I feel safe in speculating that Peter encountered the very grace of God in that room. It's possible that Jesus could have said, "I know you have rejected me, Peter, but I have not rejected you. You still have a place with me. I see your broken spirit, I've heard your cries. Surrender your heart, let me deliver you, and then go tell the world."

Grace. Undeserved love. Forgiveness.

Peter then had the choice of facing his broken life and using it for the glory of God or being like Judas and dying in his rejection. Peter chose life and life in abundance, but he had to surrender. When we choose to live in grace, we must choose to surrender to it. Whatever was said in that meeting, I believe it inspired Peter to preach his greatest sermon at Pentecost. His encounter with the grace of Jesus changed him and he was ready to shout it to the world. He was not going to be defined by his rejection of Christ; he was ready to be defined by the pursuit of grace. Freedom. At the end of Peter's surrendered life, we see compassion, we see resolve, we see peace, and we see his mission. He had a purpose, to bring others to know the grace of Christ and allow it to transform them.

This is when I began to see my story not as something to be ashamed of, but of something to minister through. There are so many hurting people who need to see the pursuing grace of God. If I kept my story to myself, then I would be masking the power of God and His ability to work in others.

This is what the Lord has called us to. We are not to proclaim the "perfection" that we display to the world, but rather our need for redemption, so that others may accept their own need. Psalm 107:2 says, "Let the redeemed of the Lord tell their story…" Our messy stories are a testimony to the world of a God working in broken people, but only if we are brave enough to proclaim it!

In learning to surrender, we must be willing to get brave, brave enough to let go of our sin, hurts, and traumas, but also our fear and pride. May the Lord strengthen our hands. There are people who may not desire our freedom and will do everything they can to enslave us.

They may judge our stories, they may condemn our stories, but in surrendering, we are choosing to no longer be held captive to shame or to the judgments of others. We are choosing life on the other side of the wall. John 8:38 says, "So if the Son sets you free, you will be free indeed." Our victory is and will always be in Jesus. Freedom.

Chapter Nine

The Proclamation

In the spirit of vulnerability, I'm going to practice it a little with you. Here's the truth: this is my first major confession of my entire story. I've mentioned it here and there to some people, but certainly not in its entirety. This is the first time I am proclaiming it. If you had asked me ten years ago if I thought I would ever write a book about my journey, I would have laughed—no cried— you out the door. First, I'm not a public person. Second, I had not experienced my grace journey yet, so I probably would have denied I had a story to share. Fortunately, the call of God leads us to places we never thought we would be. I say "fortunately" because, looking back, I am so thankful for the transformative power of God's grace. I would not be who I am today, had I not walked this road. I would not know God the way I do if He had not revealed Himself to me the way He did. I would not be writing this book, had He not inspired bravery within me. It is the pursuit of grace that transformed me, changed my mission, and caused me to act.

As I look back on this journey, I would not alter a thing, because it has led me to a deeper understanding of the character of God, and therefore has created a deeper love of the Lord. I realize that I am broken, in need, and desperate for healing, however, I also realize that because of the Lord's pursuing grace, I am fully redeemed, loved, and chosen. He has been chasing me since the day I was born, and I am so thankful to have been turned around so I could accept His outstretched arms. He chose me when I would not have chosen myself, and I am forever changed because of it.

Since beginning to write this book, the past year has been one of the most peaceful years I have had in a long time. Oh, it's absolutely chaotic with the daily adventures and demands of having four children, but my mindset is different. I see myself differently. I see my husband differently. I see my children differently. I see everyone around me differently. I've let go of the pursuit of perfection. I'm learning to embrace the mistakes, embrace the imperfections, and embrace the pursuit of grace. No longer will I live a life of having to prove my worth or seek value through the approval and actions of others. I'm living life with a different mission in my heart. I want to live a life that testifies.

In God's perfect (and humorous) ways, this year has also been one of my most challenging. I have never had so many obstacles come at me in such a short time: distractions, ruined plans, and life's dramas have been hinderances in getting any time to write. I still count myself richly blessed, but writing this book, especially toward the end, proved to be extremely difficult. Even as I am typing I can't help but chuckle at the insane number of interruptions that are taking place. Tonight, my husband bought me a hotel room so that I could escape the beautiful chaos and get a little quiet time to myself to write. Quiet is hard to come by in a family of six. As I settled in for the night, pulled my laptop to knees and began to press the keys, someone decided to pull out their bagpipes and start playing a ditty— or ten— outside my window. That is just a small, humorous taste of the challenges I have faced in trying to write this book.

As I sit on this bed, trying to pour out my heart, I realize that I am not at all surprised at the distractions that have come my way. As I said in the last chapter, when we make the decision to surrender to freedom, Satan will chase us, ready to place the chains. He does not want the message of freedom to be released. He does not want there to be hope of restoration, and he certainly does not want there to be any evidence that God has the power to work in broken people. I feel his hand against me in every way as I type out these words. Just as I have been spending this past year writing a testimony that would shout the name of Jesus, Satan has been spending this past year trying to stop me. I am not surprised at all at his attempts to bring me down. In fact, I would expect nothing less.

A few months ago, a friend who had been encouraging me as I wrote this book, sent me a message that I have kept with me throughout the writing process. She said, "Satan does not want this book to be written, does not want hope to be revealed, and does not want souls healed by Christ's love. He is going to be after you, trying to get you to doubt yourself, and who knows what else! From here on out, any doubt, fears, or unexpected drama that comes against you getting this book finished, you need to weigh with prayer. It is most likely a scheme of Satan. I would work as hard as you can to get it finished. 'Be Strong, take heart, and wait upon the Lord.' Psalms 27:14." I did not realize at the time the amount of truth she spoke. I have felt the resistance of Satan multiple times throughout this process, but here's the thing I've had to remember: the power rests with God. If it were up to my feeble mind, this would read more like a *See Spot Run* type of book. I am merely the fingers pressing the keys that God has already chosen for me to press, so if any of this book speaks to you at all, it is only by God's hand. Nothing Satan can do will ever hold any power over what the Lord can do. I must simply be strong and wait upon the Lord. If this is a message the Lord wants people to hear, then nothing will stop it. In the meantime, I'll just keep pressing the keys.

Now I feel compelled to extend to you the same message my friend sent to me. Someone somewhere needs you to tell your story. They need to hear that they are not alone. Right now, someone is out there thinking that they are the only ones who have been abused, abandoned, and broken. They are out there chasing a remedy that will never satisfy, nor heal. There are people who believe that they are the only ones who have run too far, and that grace is out of reach, and they are trying to find their place through things or people that will never give it. People are among us living lives with no hope and this will not change until we do something about it. This will not change until we begin to see the power of God working in broken people as more important than the shame of needing to be worked on. The revealing of the pursuit of grace is *vital* to a broken world; without it, the pursuit of perfection will only imprison more souls.

In living a life of testimony, you must realize that Satan will come after you. It is not an "if," but "when." As you seek to live a life of freedom he will be chasing you to imprison you to a life of shame and regret and will do everything in his power to stop you from speaking. He wants you imprisoned, he wants you to live in a life of hopelessness, and he certainly wants to prevent you from finding freedom and sharing it with the world. Please remember, life is better on the other side of the wall. Surrender yourself and speak life to anyone who will listen. Stay strong, bring the best you have to offer, and wait upon the Lord.

In the book of Malachi, we see the Lord give a challenge to the Israelites. In a time when they were called to bring Him the best of their offerings and sacrifices, they were bringing Him the defective. The Israelites were honoring the Lord with their words but held back with their actions. They were not surrendering fully to the Lord, they were holding back their best from the Lord. I cannot sit here and pretend that I do not relate to that; I do. Fear is what has held me back. What would happen if I gave the Lord what I clung to so tightly? That's exactly what the Lord wanted Israel to understand (and probably me as well.) In Malachi 3:10, the Lord gives the Israelites this challenge, "'Bring the whole tithe into the storehouse, that there may be food in my house. Test me in this, says the Lord Almighty, and see if I will not throw open the floodgates of heaven and pour out so much blessing that you will not have enough room for it.'" Here Israel receives a test. If the Israelites would be willing to give the Lord their very best, if they were willing to stop holding back, and could learn to let go, the Lord would provide His very best. There would be so much blessing there wouldn't be enough room for it. They needed to surrender their fears and give their best to the mission of the Lord, so that He could do His best in return.

The call to Israel is that same call to us today: If we surrender ourselves fully to the path of the Lord, if we no longer live in fear and hold back the best we have to offer, He will provide His best and pour out so much blessing we will not have enough room for it. Imagine the results of all of our lives surrendering to the mission of the Lord. Imagine the results of us all giving Him our very best. Surrender takes bravery. It takes self-lessness and humility, but more than anything, it takes vulnerability. It is the best sacrifice we can offer; it is giving up of ourselves for the mission of others. Surrender brings freedom, not just for us, but for the world. If we surrender everything we have, give the best we have to offer, what will the Lord provide in return? Earth-shaking results.

Isaiah was a prophet of God sent to the Israelites mostly to share warnings, but also to give hope. Isaiah says of God's mission in Isaiah 61:1-3, "He has sent me to bind up the broken-hearted, to proclaim freedom for the captives, and release from darkness for the prisoners, to proclaim the year of the Lord's favor and the day of vengeance of our God, to comfort all who mourn, and provide for those who grieve in Zion-to bestow on them a crown of beauty instead of ashes, the oil of gladness instead of mourning, and a garment of praise instead of a spirit of despair. They will be called oaks of righteousness, a planting of the Lord for the display of his splendor." It was Isaiah's mission to proclaim the Lord's message of hope to the world. It was his proclamation that would help bind up the broken, proclaim freedom for the captives, and bring beauty from ashes. His mission was to proclaim the pursuing grace of God to a broken people.

Our mission is the same as Isaiah's, and it is critical. It is the revealing of the Lord's pursuit of us that brings hope to the world. In revealing the Lord's pursuit of us, we are revealing the Lord's pursuit of others. Our testimony of transformation binds up the broken, brings gladness instead of mourning, proclaims freedom to the captives, and provides a garment of praise instead of a spirit of despair.

It is up to us to share our message of surrender, to share the message of freedom, and to reveal to the world the pursuit of grace. Satan may be running after us, but God is sprinting faster. Satan is running to destroy, but the Lord is sprinting to rebuild.

I want my life to testify to the power of God working through broken people. I want this book to testify to the power of God working through broken people, and I pray God is doing just that. It is His grace that has transformed my life and my mission. He has pursued me, redeemed me, and changed me. Sadly, many Christians are so afraid to reveal the pursuit of grace. It's embarrassing that they have to be pursued, because it means that they were once broken. It is easier and less humiliating to just stay quiet. Grace never gets proclaimed. I get it. That was me, but it is with this spirit that we withhold hope from the world. The world will not experience the transforming power of grace if we do not get brave enough to start revealing it. People cannot have their eyes opened if we are not willing to reveal what they are missing. How we live our lives testifies to the transforming power of grace, but if we stay silent, then what are we testifying to?

A life that grace transforms should look like one and sound like one. We are always testifying something about God, whether we intend to or not. Either He is a pursuer, healer, and deliverer, or He is not. Our transformed lives are the best testimony we could ever share, so to offer the pursuit of grace, we must look like we have been pursued by grace. There is no more shame, only pride that the grace of God has been extended to people like us.

This is why the story of Paul is so powerful. Paul was a Jewish man who knew the laws and prophecies of the Lord yet failed to see Christ as the fulfillment of them. In fact, in Acts 26:1-11, Paul stands before King Agrippa and confesses, "On the authority of the chief priests I put many of the saints in prison, and when they were put to death, I cast my vote against them. Many a time I went from one synagogue to another to have them punished, and I tried to force them to blaspheme. In my obsession against them, I even went to foreign cities to persecute them."

Kristen Lunceford

Not only did Paul fail to see Christ as the Messiah, but he persecuted those who did! It was only after his personal encounter with the grace of Jesus that his life was transformed. Instead of living in shame and regret, we see multiple times in the book of Acts when Paul gives his testimony to people, and the most awe-inspiring part is that he always starts with a confession of his brokenness. He starts with his failures, his persecution of others, his contempt for Christ, and lays it all out for the crowds to see. He does not hold back, he does not mince words, but chooses vulnerability, because he knows that the greatest testimony to the need of Christ is his own story.

Paul's point was, "If I can surrender, so can you! If I can be rebuilt, so can you! If grace pursued me, then how much more is grace pursuing you!" Paul chose to bring his best offering and used the ugly, messy parts of his story to provide the best God has to offer: Grace.

Paul didn't end his testimony there. He revealed the pursuit of grace that met him that life-changing day on the road to Damascus. We see in Acts 9:15 that God chooses Paul to be His instrument to the world, but to do what? The Lord tells him, "I have appeared to you to appoint you as a servant and as a witness of what you have seen of me and what I will show you. I will rescue you from your own people and from the Gentiles. I am sending you to open their eyes and turn them from darkness to light, and from the power of Satan to God, so that they may receive forgiveness of sins and a place among those who are sanctified by faith in me." Paul was being called to preach to the world that the Lord's grace was in pursuit, and Paul's life would be the revealing of it. Paul's life would become the *evidence* of a life changed by grace. He was no longer the man he used to be; he was transformed, and it was evident not just by his words, but by his rebuilt new life.

The Lord knows His pursuit of people is unrecognizable if we do not allow ourselves to see the effects of His pursuit of us. This is why Paul was so willing to repeatedly preach his redemption story. He started with the ugly and ended with the restored. In addition, he *lived* a restored life. He chose the outcasts, sat with the broken, served the poor, and preached redemption, all as a testimony to the power of his restoration. He was giving hope to a broken world, and it started with his own story. Imagine the number of people who could benefit from hearing and witnessing a testimony like that.

We know from his letters this life of testimony was not an easy road for Paul. Many doubted and were angry at his transformation, but because he was inspired by the pursuing grace of God, it didn't matter. It was his testimony, and he couldn't help but share it. In 2 Corinthians 12:9, The Lord tells Paul, "'My grace is sufficient for you, for my power is made perfect in weakness.'" No matter what others thought, no matter what others did, it was the Lord who was sustaining him in his ministry. Paul's mission had changed. I believe this is why Paul was able to say in the following verse, "Therefore I will boast all the more gladly about my weaknesses, so that Christ's power may rest on me."

Because God's grace was sufficient for Paul, he was no longer defined by his weaknesses, but rather used them as a way to point to the transformative power of Christ. In the same way, when grace becomes our identity in life, we are no longer defined by our weaknesses, but by the power of God. There is no shame in our weakness, there is no shame in our brokenness because all of it testifies to the need for grace. True transformation should produce genuine proclamation. We are no longer ashamed, but rather inspired to proclaim the pursuit of grace.

One of my favorite stories in Ezekiel is about the valley of the dry bones. Honestly, who can't relate to feeling like a valley of dry bones at one point in their life? I definitely can. In Ezekiel chapter 37, Ezekiel was brought to the middle of a desolate wasteland filled with nothing but dry bones and death. There were absolutely no signs of life, yet the Lord asked Ezekiel in verse 3, "Son of man, can these bones live?" Anyone looking at this desolate valley would testify that the life of these bones was long gone, without hope, but Ezekiel answered the Lord, "You alone know."

Ezekiel understood that the Lord sees what we cannot see. The Lord can do what we cannot do, so he let the power rest where it should, and God delivered. In verse 5 the Lord said to the bones, "I will make breath enter you and you will come to life. I will attach tendons to you and make flesh come upon you and cover you with skin; I will put breath in you, and you will come to life. Then you will know that I am the Lord." The bones came together, the tendons grew, flesh appeared, then the Lord entered these lifeless bodies and breathed life into them. That's the transformative power of the Lord.

This is our message. This is what we proclaim with our stories. It is when our bones are dried up and our hope is gone, that we testify to the One who breathes life. We can speak the message of life with our words to those who need it the most, but it is our *revival* that proclaims the loudest. Are we willing to live a life of testimony of the God who breathes life into our dry bones? Do we look alive? Do we look restored? Do we look redeemed?

Living in grace should not only produce a proclamation of grace, but a life that reveals it. Charles Spurgeon says, "If grace does not make us differ from other men, it is not the grace which God gives his elect," (see Ellis, 2010). If our lives do not testify to the pursuit of grace, then perhaps we have not truly accepted it. Perhaps we are still living in the pursuit of perfection. When we choose to accept the pursuit of God, our lives will look different because of it. We will look and act as if life has been breathed into our very selves.

When we think back at stories I've mentioned in this book like David, the Samaritan woman, Peter, and Paul, we see that their encounters with the grace of God affected them and changed them. Everything they had been living for, everything that they believed had sustained them flipped. They were completely transformed people. The transformation of their lives became further testimony to the words they were preaching.

Unfortunately, there have been many times in my life when I have witnessed a life transformed by grace that surrenders to the idea that a transformation is no longer essential. It is a sad but true reality. Living a transformed life can become a burden to some, because we are so easily drawn back into our old ways of living. We forget what grace has done for us, so it becomes easy for us to let it go. Notice that I said *we* let go. Remember that grace is always in pursuit, it is we who have the choice to embrace it.

The entire cycle of the Israelites points to this very idea. For over a thousand years the Israelites lived in the cycle of seeking their own deliverance through things or people that could not provide it, eventually realized their failure and brokenness, accepted the Lord's grace, which produced short term transformation, only to turn around and reject the Lord once again to return to their old ways of living. It's the cycle of humanity. We're never content. We are always on the lookout for something that could provide more, deliver more, or satisfy more. So how can we learn to be satisfied with the grace of God, thrive in the transformation, and continue to reveal hope to the world?

I believe the first step is to get vocal. We don't necessarily have to shout our testimony of redemption to the world, although I'm certainly not opposed to it, but we could absolutely share it with it a neighbor or a friend. We could share it with our children. We could look for broken people sitting next to us in the pews and share our message of transforming grace, offering hope to anyone in need of it. When we share the pursuit of grace then it is always on our minds, always on our hearts, and always on the tips of our tongues. It is a daily reminder of what we're living for. Deuteronomy 4:9 says, "Only be careful, and watch yourselves closely so that you do not forget the things your eyes have seen or let them slip from your heart as long as you live. Teach them to your children and to their children after them." To end the pursuit of perfection, we must proclaim the pursuit of grace, and when we are constantly testifying to the pursuit of grace, we are constantly reminded of it.

The next step is to get mission-minded. Changing our focus to being intentional with *living* the testimony of grace is vital. We must seek out the outcasts, the hurting and the broken and make them our daily mission. The life changes that happen when we become intentional in seeking out the hurting are incredible. Nothing seems to anger us quite as much, self-righteousness seems to fade away, and difficult people are seen as opportunities to show the love of Christ.

What I think so many people are drawn to about Christ is that He was intentional in seeking out the outcasts. His pride was the least of His concerns in dealing with broken people. He ate with them, touched them, heard their cries, and healed their wounds. He wanted to live out grace and sought opportunities to do so. We should do the same. Think of the impact we could have on the world if we all sought out the opportunities to show grace as Christ did. It's time to get intentional. It's time to get mission-minded. It's time to set the captives free.

When I look back over the past nine months of writing this book, I am in awe of the power of God working in all of it. I can see the journey He has taken me on and the people He has brought into my life to bring this to fruition. I am forever grateful for the people surrounding me who have been willing to share their testimony to the pursuit of grace. It takes bravery to be vulnerable. It takes humility. It takes strength that only God can give. I am forever changed because of them and the hope that they provided to a broken person like me. It was witnessing the power of God in them that gave me hope of the power of God working in me.

The people in this book who have shared their stories are people sitting in the pews next to us. I pray that is a comfort for you, but I also pray that it is a challenge to you. We, as a church, must step up and start to edify each other. Life gets hard. Situations get messy. We get lonely. The church is the Lord's remedy to that. Galatians 6 calls us to carry each other's burdens. As a church, we must throw off the temptation of perfectionism, step off the pedestals, and begin to carry the loads. We must dig deep roots, see people as they are, and use our stories as a testimony of grace.

Paul wrote to the church in Corinth, "Praise be to the God and Father our Lord Jesus Christ, the Father of compassion and the God of all comfort who comforts us in all our troubles, so that we can comfort those in any trouble with the comfort we ourselves received from God. For just as the sufferings of Christ flow over into our lives, so also through Christ our comfort overflows." We are called to bring comfort into the lives of others by sharing the very comfort given to us. Satan thrives on our silence. Satan thrives on hopelessness. I pray that together we can get brave. I pray that together we can break off the chains, step into freedom, and proclaim it to the world.

A few weeks ago, my sweet friend Erin sent me this passage as a prayer for the ones reading this book. I am writing it out in this chapter because I believe the power of so many of us praying this prayer together could be earth- shaking. I pray that you believe so, too. It is from Psalm 51:5-19, The Passion translation.

> Lord, I have been a sinner from birth, from the moment my mother conceived me. I know that you delight to set your truth deep in my spirit.
>
> So come into the hidden places of my heart and teach me wisdom. Purify my conscience! Make this leper clean again! Wash me in your love until I am pure in heart. Satisfy me in your sweetness, and my song of joy will return.
>
> The places you have crushed within me will rejoice in your healing touch. Hide my sins from your face; erase all my guilt by your saving grace.
>
> Keep creating in me a clean heart. Fill me with pure thoughts and holy desires, ready to please you. May you never reject me! May you never take from me your sacred spirit!
>
> Let my passion for life be restored, tasting joy in every breakthrough you bring to me. Hold me close to you with a willing spirit that obeys whatever you say.
>
> Then I can show other guilty ones how loving and merciful you are. They will find their way back home to you, knowing that you will forgive them.
>
> O God, my saving, God, deliver me fully from every sin, even the sin that brought bloodguilt. Then my heart will once again be thrilled to sing the passionate songs of joy and deliverance. Lord God, unlock my heart, unlock my lips, and I will overcome with my joyous praise! For the source of your pleasure is not in my performance or the sacrifices I might offer to you. The fountain of

your pleasure is found in the sacrifice of my shattered heart before you. You will not despise my tenderness as I bow down humbly at your feet… And when we are fully restored, you will rejoice and take delight in every offering of our lives as we bring our sacrifices of righteousness before you in love.

Amen.

My dear readers, my prayer for us is that we are ready to surrender, ready to be rebuilt, and no longer ashamed of the power of God working in us. I pray that we look at our broken lives as opportunities to testify of a God who is in constant pursuit. May we be intentional in living out a grace-centered mission and break the chains of perfection. The world is in desperate need of it.

I pray with all my heart that you are able to accept the pursuing arms of grace, be transformed, and then reveal it to the world. Do not let shame overtake you. Do not be overcome with fear. Instead, let us cause the earth to tremble with our shouts of redemption and healing. Let us forever proclaim the pursuit of grace.

Notes

Chapter 1

p. 18 Liles, Maryn. "50 Brene Brown Quotes for Powerful Motivation," Readers Digest, April 12, 2022, www.rd.com/article/brene-brown

Chapter 3

p. 41 Rodin, Dr. Scott. "Grace Undeserved" The Steward's Journey www.thestewardsjourney.com

p. 42 Taylor, Justin. "J. I. Packer on Something More Important Than Knowing God," The Gospel Coalition, June 6, 2016, www.thegospelcoalition.org

Chapter 5

p. 59 Cohen, Sandy. "Suicide Rates Highest Among Teens and Adults." UCLA Health. March 15, 2022. https://uclahealth.org

p. 60 Carnazzi, Stefano. "Kintsugi: The Art of Precious Scars." Lifegate. January 30, 2016. https://www.lifegate.com/kintsugi

Chapter 6

p. 73 Babu, Chaya. "Name Changers: 285 Indian Girls No Longer 'Unwanted'. NBC News. October 22, 2011. https://nbcnews.com/id/wbna44998378

Kristen Lunceford

p. 77 Ten Boom, Corrie. "Guideposts Classics: Corrie Ten Boom on Forgiveness." November 1972. https://guideposts.org/positive-living/guideposts-classics-corrie-ten-boom-forgiveness/

Chapter 9

p. 116 Ellis, Paul. "None but Jesus! Spurgeon on Grace." Escape to Reality. November 15, 2010.
www.escapetoreality.org/2010/11/15spurgeon-on-grace/

About Kharis Publishing:

Kharis Publishing, an imprint of Kharis Media LLC, is a leading Christian and inspirational book publisher based in Aurora, Chicago metropolitan area, Illinois. Kharis' dual mission is to give voice to under-represented writers (including women and first-time authors) and equip orphans in developing countries with literacy tools. That is why, for each book sold, the publisher channels some of the proceeds into providing books and computers for orphanages in developing countries so that these kids may learn to read, dream, and grow. For a limited time, Kharis Publishing is accepting unsolicited queries for nonfiction (Christian, self-help, memoirs, business, health and wellness) from qualified leaders, professionals, pastors, and ministers. Learn more at: https://kharispublishing.com/